MW00596617

PAULINE

PRAISE FOR LONNIE DUSTIN

"*The Haughtons* is a compelling story of family dynamics with love, power, deceit, and loss spanning generations It proves our choices can have lasting consequences felt through the layers of family. Lonnie Dustin captivates the reader by weaving a tale in and out of time."

— *ABBIGAIL RILEY, EDUCATOR, TEXAS*

A Family Saga Destined for Success!"

Lonnie Dustin has created a page turning saga bringing much enjoyment in its tale of good and evil. Its characters are either guided by their faith or, in some cases, truly misguided in their actions. So complex are two characters, Lonnie has written two separate books to reveal what makes them the most unlikeable people they are! The second and third books will be published in the near future. I am certain they will be a must read!

— *MARK MCMORROW, CURATOR OF THE JOAN COLLINS ARCHIVE, WWW.JOANCOLLINSARCHIVE.BLOGSPOT.COM; JOAN COLLINS OFFICIAL SITE HTTP://WWW. JOANCOLLINS.COM*

ALSO BY LONNIE DUSTIN

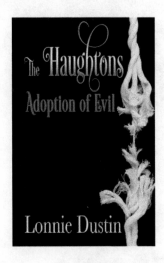

The Haughtons Adoption of Evil

Book II of The Haughtons

Pauline

Lonnie Dustin

PAULINE: BOOK II OF THE HAUGHTONS

Copyright © 2023 by Lonnie Dustin

Cover Copyright © 2023 by Lonnie Dustin

All rights reserved.

Published by Luv'n Liv'n

Editing Services, Formatting, and Cover Design by Stacey Smekofske at EditsByStacey.com

The Haughtons is a work of fiction, inspired by life experiences but not representative of identifiable individuals. Some names and identifying details have been changed to protect the privacy of individuals.

No part of this book may be reproduced in any form or by any electronic or mechanical means, including information storage and retrieval systems, without written permission from the author, except for the use of brief quotations in a book review.

Identifiers:

Paperback 978-1-958314-05-0

Hardcover 978-1-958314-06-7

eBook 978-1-958314-04-3

Audio Book 978-1-958314-07-4

For my Family

CONTENTS

NOTE FROM THE AUTHOR

The successes of the fictional Haughton family were based upon the principles and the vision of one man, Benjamin Haughton. The Sacred Thread he wove became a lifeline for all who would take hold. Faith, integrity, responsibility, commitment, servitude, generosity, humility, and most importantly, love are woven together, protected and repaired when necessary, to provide strength in family, friendships and business associations.

Pauline Bianchi had no such lifeline. In solitude, she struggled to survive the onslaught of those whom she should have been able to trust, those from whom she should have gained her strength.

As I wrote Pauline, I recognized many similarities between her experiences and those experiences of my own. I recognized the perilous results I could have suffered had I not been offered a lifeline, a Sacred Thread.

There are those whom destiny appears to have smitten with an impossible plight, those for whom the struggle to survive appears unsurmountable, unforgiving, and unending. There are also those who silently feel the relentless burden of obscurity and of hopelessness. They may not live in squaller, they may not appear in need, but they too desperately need a lifeline of hope.

Is there redemption? Is such a thought or such an experience offered to all?

The answers to these questions and so many more are offered in the pages you are about to read. As you read Pauline, I encourage you to refer back to my first book, Adoption of Evil. There are numerous hidden gems to be discovered between the two books. Dates, names, and locations provide hidden meanings throughout each book.

The irony is intentional—such is life.

Lonnie Dustin

PREFACE

I was met with a gentle smile, a firm handshake, and a light chuckle.

I thanked him for purchasing *The Haughtons: Adoption of Evil* and for his invitation to chat over a cup of coffee.

"I can't even begin to tell you how shocked Carrie and I were when we read your note," I said, smiling.

"I can imagine you were. I'm sorry about that. The note wasn't meant to be seen by anyone in particular. It certainly wasn't my intention to shock you or your wife, Mr. Dustin."

I loosened my grip, but he continued to shake my hand. His penetrating stare made the greeting awkward.

"And I want you to know, it isn't my intention to interrupt your life," he added as our hands dropped to our sides.

"So, here we are; what now?"

"Mr. Dustin. I want to give you some information you may not have known when you wrote your book. Believe me, I'm not excusing her actions or the abuses you and your wife suffered because of her son. I just want you to hear the whole story."

He paused to gather his thoughts. Then he chuckled. "Heck, I don't know. Maybe I am making excuses for her—a little." He appeared momentarily lost in reflective thought.

My head unintentionally nodded in affirmation.

He continued, "It's hard for me to think of her the way you've portrayed her, Mr. Dustin. Please, don't misunderstand me. Your accounts of her actions are probably accurate, but did you ever consider why she was the way she was?"

The question irked me. "To be perfectly honest, I really didn't care *why*—never gave it a thought. I mean, I don't want to sound heartless, but when you are going through hell, why take time to monitor the temperature?"

"I understand; I get it. I just want to make certain you hear the whole story."

It was obvious—*he was excusing her!* We'd just sat down, and I was already feeling defensive. I thought to myself: *you want me to hear the whole story—what are you talking about? I wrote the story! We lived the story; we're still living the story!* The nerve of this guy. I tried to sound calm. "Frankly, and again, I don't mean to sound heartless, but I don't want to dredge up the past any more than I would ever want to relive it. For my family, the story is written, the book is finished, case closed."

He did not respond. He sat across from me as if waiting for me to unburden myself of my emotions.

So, I continued. "It was a painful time, a frightening time. The stresses my wife suffered were immeasurable—not to mention the heartbreak. Why on earth should I care about what influenced the woman? We've all faced challenges in our lives. We've all made mistakes—some of us, serious mistakes. Not everyone chooses to become so hateful. Not everyone makes it their life's ambition to hurt others. The woman was jealous, selfish, and evil!"

He took a sip of his coffee and appeared to be giving his response careful consideration before speaking. "Mr. Dustin, I suppose from your account, Pauline became all of those things." He took another sip, and as he looked at the ceiling, he continued. "There was a time, however, when she was just a little girl." His upward gaze slowly returned to me. "Have you thought about that? Have you considered the fact Pauline was once a vulnerable child—perhaps herself the unfortunate victim of everything she became?"

Oh, Dear Lord, what did I get myself into? I thought.

CHAPTER ONE
BUNNY EARS
JANUARY 1948

"No, Pauline! Bunny ears. BUNNY EARS! Pay attention. You're not paying attention! Now listen to me—watch. You pull both strings so that they are the same length!"

Tears blurred Pauline's vision. She dropped the string in her left hand to wipe her eyes. Instantaneously, she felt a strike to the back of her head.

"No, you idiot! Hold on to both strings; and stop your sniveling! You keep those strings the same length or so help me I'll... Pay attention! You'll never learn if you don't pay attention and follow directions!"

Trying to see was useless. Pauline's eyes had filled once again with tears. She struggled not to blink, fearing the tears would fall on her glistening patent leather shoes—once again, unleashing her mother's fury.

Bunny ears; BUNNY EARS! Pauline thought.

Slowly, carefully, calculating every move—rehearsing each move in her mind before proceeding—she made a loop in both strings. It was then she felt the second blow of her mother's open palm against the back of her head. The impact instantly atomized the droplets still clinging to Pauline's eyelashes. To her horror, a thin layer of moisture instantly fogged the mirrored reflection in her patent leather shoes.

"Now see what you've done? IDIOTA!"

Pauline struggled through the fear to remember. Hold one string in each hand, make a cross with one string over the other, halfway up the other string, and wrap the top string over and around the string that is underneath—the string slipped from the tiny fingers of her right hand.

"Idiot! It is NOT that difficult! *Sei nato solo per tormentarmi?*" (You were only born to torment me?)

Pauline took a deep breath and began her third attempt. Again, she rehearsed every move. Hold one string in each hand and make a cross with one string over the other. Halfway up the other string, wrap the top string over and around the string that is underneath. Now pull both loops.

There was complete silence. Pauline's jaw dropped. She was afraid to move. Would the laces come untied if she let go? She stared at the loops—they seemed to be secure. Was it possible? Pauline's heart raced as she thought, *perhaps I did it!*

Her white fingers grasped onto both loops as she raised her head and eyes to meet her mother's gaze, hoping to find approval.

Instead, she was met with a stern glare. "It's about time!"

Pauline immediately returned her attention to the two strings she held in her hands. Her mother, Elizabeth, shook her head in disgust and stomped out of Pauline's bedroom, slamming the door behind her. For the moment, Pauline was safe. She prayed her mother would never return!

Pauline firmly held the bunny ears in her grasp. Slowly, cautiously, she loosened her grip. To her amazement, the laces held firm. Her shoe was tied! Self-doubt was replaced by pride. She'd done it; she'd done it! Pauline quickly reached for the strings on her left shoe, but they were not the same length. They were supposed to be the same length! Something was wrong—this wasn't fair! Her mother left a six-inch string on one side of the shoe and a three-inch string on the other. Pauline felt heat radiate from her heart outward; her face felt hot.

She glared at the woman beyond her bedroom door. *I hate you! I hate you! You were born only to torment me.*

Pauline's muscles quivered as she struggled to remove the entire string from her untied shoe. Suddenly, she realized she could make the strings the same length by loosening the shoe and slowly pulling the shorter string, allowing the length to follow. After several attempts, the right and left strings were the same lengths.

The room spun as Pauline wondered if she would remember. Did the uneven strings erase her memory of the bunny ears? She prayed —she prayed—and she practiced. Over and over again, Pauline practiced tying her shoe. *Over, around, under, pull; bunny-ear, bunny-ear; over around under pull;* SUCCESS!

Her tummy jumped with excitement. She was doing it all by herself! She quickly turned toward the closed door, momentarily desiring to leap from her bed and fling herself into the arms of a proud and loving mother. Instinctively, Pauline stopped. She lived with no such woman. There would be no open arms, no pride. Pauline was safer staying in her room with her twin Duchess Dolls and Little Golden Books. Daddy would be home soon. Daddy would understand. He would share the excitement; Daddy was always excited, always proud, and always loving. When Daddy came home, Pauline's longing heart would be satisfied.

───────────────

His knock at the door was unmistakable. Shave *and a haircut, five bits!*

"Hello?" he sang as he opened the door and peered into what seemed to be an empty room. "Where is my Princess? Are you hiding? Alas, fair maiden, you cannot hide from me!"

Pauline's muffled giggle came from behind the bedroom door as she held both hands over her mouth—trying not to give away her whereabouts.

Pauline watched his tall, thin frame slowly, stealthily creep into her room. He was her knight in shining armor, the most handsome man in the world! His hair was thick, dark, and wavy. Pauline studied his features. She knew every crevasse in his chiseled face. While she watched from behind the door, he stood in the middle of the room and perused all her potential hiding places. He moved first to Pauline's chest of drawers. Pauline giggled uncontrollably once again.

How silly, she thought. *I can't fit in those drawers.* But her father was careful to open every single drawer, checking under sweaters, pants, and pajamas. It was a routine he and Pauline rehearsed often. Pauline cherished and looked forward to the comedy. He had come home to rescue her!

Having completed his search through each drawer, Pauline's father turned with a puzzled look on his face. "Hmm; you are not in there. I thought for certain you would be tucked away under a warm sweater."

Pauline once again tightened her grip across her mouth.

"AH! I know—in the closet!" He opened the closet door and shouted, "Gotcha!" as if expecting to see Pauline. Again, his search was foiled.

"All right, my beautiful rose, I have you now. You must be under your bed!" He got on his hands and knees, folded back the bedspread, and peered under the suspended box spring. Just then, Pauline dashed from behind the bedroom door and jumped on his back.

"Oh, my! Oh, my! You've got me! Whatever shall I do? I am your faithful servant, your highness!"

Pauline was too excited to continue her welcome home vignette. "Oh, Daddy! Daddy, look what I've done! Look what I've done, Daddy. And I did it all by myself!" She loosened her grip from around his neck, slid off his back, and stood proudly in front of her father.

"Rosebud! You, you tied your shoes? Did you really? REALLY? Oh, my goodness! You tied your shoes? Oh, dear Lord. What has become of my little girl? She is growing up too fast!"

"I can do it again for you, Daddy. I can do it again!"

"Sweetheart, would you do that for me, please?"

Pauline jumped up on the edge of the bed. Frank was still in front of her on his knees. She pulled her left knee to her chest and loosened the ties of that shoe. She was so excited to loosen the ties on her right shoe the left shoe fell to the floor.

Her father picked up the left shoe as Pauline's focus was on the two strings of her right shoe in her hand. He studied her face as her eyes focused with absolute determination. His heart swelled with pride at the picture of angelic passion.

There was no hesitation. Pauline tied the right shoe. A smile spread across her cheeks. She reached out and grabbed the left shoe from her dad's hand. Her hands moved swiftly as she tied her left shoe with total confidence.

"THERE!"

Pauline had done it. Frank swept her into his arms and twirled her around the room in joyful celebration!

"Oh, my goodness. That is wonderful. How in the world did you learn to tie your shoes?"

Before Pauline had a chance to share her story, Elizabeth interrupted from the doorway. "She learned because her mother spent the better part of the morning fighting with her to pay attention to instructions! I'm telling you, Frank, if you don't do something to discipline your daughter, we're going to be struggling with a delinquent later on!"

Still kneeling on the floor in front of Pauline, Frank slowly set Pauline back on the bed. He turned, making sure he shielded Pauline from his emotions, which were ignited by Elizabeth's interruption. He bit his lip—holding back his anger.

"Liz, come with me for a moment. I'd like to talk with you in the other room."

Frank turned back to Pauline and gave her a squeeze, a wink, and a kiss on the forehead. In an exuberant whisper and with a second loving squeeze, he said, "You are amazing! I am so proud of what you did. Congratulations, Rosebud!"

Nothing could spoil the sense of belonging radiating from her father.

Nothing could mistake the animus emitting from her mother.

In the other room, Frank purposefully began, "Elizabeth, I'm going to make this very simple for you. Don't ever make our daughter feel small. If you have nothing positive to say, say nothing! Don't put in our daughter's head what you think she will be or won't be later in life—and do not chastise me in front of her for not being the parent you think she needs! My relationship with our daughter will not be diminished while you continually distance yourself with your harsh tongue!"

Elizabeth was never one to back down. Her onslaught was just beginning. "Sure! Go ahead, big man. Talk your talk. You're not the one staying at home listening to her whining all day." She puffed up her chest, stuck out her chin, and mockingly swaggered up to her husband. "Go ahead, Mr. Big Shot, Mr. Professional Businessman. You go and have your fancy lunches and drinks. Leave all the discipline to me—make me the bad guy while you come home and are lavished with a warm meal and hugs and kisses from *that little brat!*" Elizabeth's voice reached a crescendo when she spoke in Italian that neighbors in the adjacent townhouses could hear. "Get it through your head, big man—you're creating a problem child. It's you! Look in the mirror, big shot. One day, you'll get it through that thick Sicilian skull of yours—she isn't the perfect child you make her out to be!"

Frank's shoulders sank. He was too verbally beaten to find strength for a continued argument. His shoulders dropped. His long lanky arms lifelessly hung at his sides. "Why do you carry on like this, Elizabeth? She is just a child; you're the adult. You're the one who needs to set an example."

Elizabeth turned her back and stormed toward the kitchen. Her arms flayed over her head. The dishtowel she held scattered family pictures along the long, narrow hallway. *"Sei un idiota! I don't know why I ever married you."*

Watching her storm out of the bedroom and into the kitchen, Frank Bianchi thought to himself in Italian, *I have often wondered that, my dear, often I have wondered.*

CHAPTER TWO
I GET IT
JANUARY 2023

"Look, I get it—Pauline had a rough childhood. I'm sorry to hear it but, once again, a lot of very good, very productive people make it through horrible childhoods." I said while looking at the last sip of my coffee.

He gave no response.

I took a sip. "How did you know Pauline?"

"I didn't. Through a series of unintended circumstances, I came in contact with her younger sister, Peggy."

"And that's where you got your information?" I adjusted myself in my seat and searched for the server with the needed refill.

"Yes—for the most part." He paused. "Pauline told her sister everything. Peggy was Pauline's only lifeline to her past. Having established a relationship with Peggy, I also met with others who grew up with Pauline. They were very open and positive about their experiences with her until...," he sighed, "until she went away."

"Went away?" I asked.

"I'll get to that. Much of what you wrote about Pauline eerily mirrors what I was told her mother was like. Her mother loved being the center of attention, on her terms, without commitments."

I had to chuckle. "Heredity."

"No," he shook his head. "I don't think so."

He looked around, hoping for that refill as well.

"Pauline's mother didn't pass her personality on to Pauline—not genetically, anyway. No other person in the family had those traits. From what I was told, Pauline's older brother was a prince of a man. Everyone spoke of him with great admiration and pride."

"Pauline never spoke of her family. Come to think of it, I don't remember her talking about her past at all," I said.

He didn't immediately respond. I took another sip, raised an eyebrow, and tilted my head in his direction to signal it was his serve.

CHAPTER THREE
LOST KEYS
MAY 1948

"Pauline? Pauline, have you seen my keys?" Douglas called from his bedroom. "I thought I put them right here on my dresser."

Douglas was ten years Pauline's senior, and he was like a second father to her. He too was Pauline's hero.

Pauline sheepishly appeared in Douglas's doorway, "Uh-uh." Douglas paused for a moment, staring inquisitively at his younger sister. Pauline drew both thumbs up to her lips and nervously twisted her body from side to side. She fought to keep her eyes from meeting his—a dead giveaway!

"Pauline, are you sure?" Douglas suspiciously prodded.

Pauline giggled. She couldn't restrain herself any longer. She turned abruptly and ran from Douglas's doorway, down the hall to her bedroom. She could feel the vibration of her brother's footsteps on the wood slat floors as he closed in behind her. Pauline squealed in delightful fear. She darted into her room, hoping to close and lock the door behind her—it was too late! A large open palm met the closing door. Then came the deep, sinister growl. Pauline covered her eyes and screamed.

Douglas swept Pauline up in his arms and tossed her onto her bed. The tickling was almost too much for Pauline to take. She tried to tell Douglas where his keys were, but her laughter would not allow her to breathe. Formulating words was impossible.

"Had enough? Had enough, you little munchkin?" Douglas paused momentarily from his tickling torture to allow Pauline to respond.

"I give; I give, Douglas," Pauline screamed through her laughter. "They're in the laundry basket!" Pauline pleaded for mercy.

Not willing to leave the room without Pauline, Douglas once again heaved her over his shoulder. Pauline continued to giggle uncontrollably as he playfully tickled her while carrying her down the hallway and whisking her into the laundry room.

The tickling stopped as Douglas put Pauline down and slowly opened the basket lid. Just as she'd said, the keys were in the basket, resting on top of the morning shower towels. Douglas swept her up in his arms and hugged her. "You found them! How can I thank you?"

"I love you, Douglas," Pauline quietly whispered.

"And I love you, munchkin," Douglas replied as he kissed her cheek.

Doug, as his friends called him, was a thoughtful, compassionate young man. He was selfless in his attitude toward others, always willing to help—he was, however, uncomfortable with the attention his gracious demeanor often brought him.

The firstborn of the Bianchi children, Douglas witnessed, and often experienced, the verbal attacks of his mother. Much like his father, Douglas was the strong, quiet type, but he was by no means shy. He had his own challenges with his mother and carefully picked his battles. A quick wit, Douglas was usually capable of controlling situations without confrontation. He keenly understood his mother's obsession with status. She needed to be needed—until someone needed her. For as long as Doug could remember, his father endured her relentless sharp tongue of criticism, but his father never lost his temper. He was a man of immense patience—too much, Doug thought. Within his father's patience, there was a quiet strength Douglas wished to emulate. It would become one of his most indomitable qualities.

Doug put his keys in his pocket and retrieved his jacket from the closet. Pauline asked, "Where ya going, Doug?" Doug could sense the sadness in Pauline's voice.

"I've gotta get to work, munchkin. Maybe Mom will bring you to the store, and I can see you there."

"She won't take me. She'll take Peggy. She takes Peggy everywhere; it's not fair. I always have to stay home by myself." Pauline lamented.

"You don't always stay by yourself." Doug's eyes stared into space for a moment before he suddenly lunged toward Pauline and resumed his tickling. "Sometimes you have *me* to contend with!" It was enough of a distraction to temporarily ease Pauline's hurt feelings.

CHAPTER FOUR

THE CONVERSATION CONTINUES

"I knew Pauline had a brother but never heard much about him. Like I said, Pauline spoke very little about anyone in her family. It was as if she didn't have a past." I spoke in a flat voice and leaned back in my chair.

"And that's my point! Pauline never referred to her past because Pauline was continually running from it. She once told Peggy everything she'd ever had, everyone she'd ever known, ever cared for, had been taken away."

"Ah, come on," I said. "She had a home—a family. She grew up after the war when everyone was rebuilding. Everyone was hopeful. The fact that she chose to be negative didn't absolve her of her responsibility to contribute."

His face contorted as he once again shook his head. "I don't think you can so quickly place that responsibility on her. Remember, we're talking about a child, not the woman you knew."

CHAPTER FIVE
DUTY CALLS
MARCH 1951

Douglas was the first home. He stopped at the mailbox, grabbed the mail, entered the kitchen through the back door, and tossed the mail on the countertop. Turning to walk to his room, he halted when one of the letters caught his attention. He reached for the letter and read the address.

Selective Service Department of the United States of America
Mr. Douglas Bianchi
9 Warren Street, Jamesburg, NJ

Douglas took a deep breath. If this was what he thought it was. His plans for advancement at the Williamstown Foundry would be temporarily placed on hold. Douglas hesitantly opened the envelope and unfolded the letter.

SELECTIVE SERVICE SYSTEM
Local Board No. 16
ORDER TO REPORT FOR INDUCTION

The President of the United States

March 15, 1951
To Douglas Bianchi

Greetings:
You are hereby ordered for induction into the Armed Forces
of the United States and to report at 1200, April 17, 1951, for
transportation to an Armed Forces Induction Station.

B. Blankenship
B. Blankenship Member
Executive Secretary, Local Board

Douglas's hands trembled. He read the letter again, not fully
believing what he'd just read. He reached for the envelope without
looking away from the letter. The envelope slipped from his fingertips and fell into the sink. Douglas temporarily escaped the letter to
retrieve the envelope from the sink. There was no mistake; it was
addressed to Douglas Bianchi. Douglas slowly walked into the living
room holding both the envelope and the notice.

Conscription was not foreign to Douglas. Several of his friends
had received notification and were now the property of the United
States of America's Military Forces.

Images of combat raced through his mind. Douglas had always
boasted of being a patriot. This notification tested his metal.
Standing along West Railroad Boulevard and waving the flag while
cheering the marching lines of enlisted men on Independence Day
was one thing, but becoming one of them, heads shaved, uniforms
pressed, and emotionless stares was quite another.

A myriad of questions whizzed through his mind. With every
question, Douglas's conclusion remained the same: "I am in the military. My life is not my own. I must fight for my country and endeavor
to return safely to it."

The slamming of the kitchen screen door startled Douglas, who was still transfixed in the imagery the letter had inspired.

"Hello, honey. How was work today?" Elizabeth called from the kitchen.

Douglas did not know how to answer. The day had been relatively uneventful. Had he known his civilian days were limited, he would have made certain this one was far more memorable.

"Douglas?" Elizabeth walked from the kitchen into the living room. "Douglas, did you hear me?"

Douglas was still unable to form words enough to engage in conversation. He looked up from the notification in his right hand and the envelope in his left. Elizabeth stopped mid-stride.

"What is it, Douglas?" She ran to his side and reached for the notification. As her eyes skimmed the notification, the realization struck her. "Oh, dear God. NO!" Elizabeth cried. "No, no, no! Douglas, there must be some mistake. This isn't right. You're just a boy; my boy. No! Douglas, this just cannot be!" Elizabeth walked past Douglas and fell onto the sofa, holding the letter in her hand. She read it again. "Douglas, honey. We'll work something out; we'll find a way." She paused and in disbelief continued, "No! No, this just cannot be!"

Elizabeth's sudden dramatic response pulled Douglas from his inner turmoil, and he shamefully recognized his own timorous reaction to the notification. "No, Mother. No. I have been called to serve my country, and I will do so with pride and patriotic resolve," Douglas firmly stated.

"Absolutely not, Douglas! I will not have it!" Elizabeth insisted.

"Mother! I'm the one who has been called by my country to serve —and I will serve! The letter was not written to you! Your name does not appear anywhere in the letter. No one is asking your permission! Stop interfering with my life!"

The exchange briefly averted his attention from reality. His life was about to change forever.

Elizabeth made no attempt to argue further. She shook her head in quiet opposition to the notice she still clutched. The longer she sat, the more vociferously her head shook until she bolted from the sofa and into her bedroom.

Douglas could hear her crying through the closed door. Her sobs gave him a strange sense of satisfaction. Perhaps she possessed a modicum of love.

CHAPTER SIX
SPARKING MY INTEREST

"Do you mind if I take some notes?" I asked.

"Please do," he responded. He waited for me to get out my notebook before continuing. "Pauline's mother was verbally abusive. She was careful not to expose this part of her personality to the public, but her harshness behind the closed doors of their home was relentless. No one could give me an explanation for it. My guess is she couldn't stand the competition."

"Competition?"

"Sure. While she was pregnant, Elizabeth was the belle of the ball. Once she gave birth, she became a supporting actress, and her children were the stars. Elizabeth was unwilling to share the spotlight with anyone."

"And no one caught on?" I scribbled on the pad to get the ink to flow.

"To the outside observer, she was a wonderful mother. Anyone suspecting otherwise feared her sharp and unbridled tongue. Her retribution was well rehearsed—calculated. She had an uncanny way of insulting someone and making them feel responsible."

"Sounds familiar." I pressed the pen on the pad, and the information flowed at the same pace as the ink.

CHAPTER SEVEN

THE DANCE ACADEMY

APRIL 1952

Elizabeth gathered Peggy's costumes and made her way to the car. It was Peggy's first troupe recital, and Elizabeth wanted everything to flow flawlessly.

"Pauline. Pauline, honey. Get Peggy's Carryall on my dresser for me. Be careful with it. Don't hold it by the chain; keep it flat for me, baby."

Her mother's saccharin tone put Pauline on guard. Before taking it to the car, Pauline gathered Peggy's Carryall and set it on her mother's bed. As she carefully opened the sculpted poplar box, a perfumed powder puff filled the room with the fragrance of fresh-cut roses. She smiled and closed the lid, proudly imagining the judges' faces as Peggy performed her tap and ballet numbers.

"Thank you, baby," Elizabeth responded as Pauline brought the box from the house to the car. Peggy was already seated in the front seat of their 1949 Dodge Custom Town sedan. Elizabeth smiled with pride, gently pinching Peggy's cheeks. "Oooh, you are going to be just wonderful! Mommy is so proud of you!" Peggy giggled.

Pauline stood behind her mother and quietly smiled. She too was proud of Peggy, but her heart longed for a quality of her own, an ability her mother would equally appreciate and boast about.

"Get in the car, Pauline. I've got to get the brownies." Elizabeth hustled into the house.

Pauline struggled to open the heavy back seat door and took her place directly behind her sister.

Their mother returned with the freshly baked brownies. "Are we ready, girls?" Elizabeth joyfully asked.

"I'm ready, Mommy," Peggy replied.

"Are you scared, Peggy?" Pauline innocently asked.

Elizabeth immediately became ridged. Gazing into the rearview mirror, Pauline realized she'd said something terribly wrong. Her mother's searing stare caused her to recoil deep within the cushion of the back seat.

"Don't you EVER ask your sister a question like that!" Elizabeth scolded. "Your sister has no reason to be nervous. She is an excellent dancer, better than any girl her age." Elizabeth glared into the rearview mirror. "... OR OLDER!"

Pauline understood her mother's veiled message. Her scolding cut deep. "I was just—" Pauline began to explain.

"You were just being a jealous little imp!" Elizabeth interrupted. "Just sit still and be quiet! I want your sister to relax and enjoy this afternoon!"

Pauline knew better than to say another word. Being quiet would be her safest option.

Elizabeth reached over and patted Peggy's leg, making certain her effusive response to Peggy was evident to Pauline. "We are going to be wonderful today. Aren't we, baby? Mommy loves you very much."

Jonesby Dance Academy was one of twenty-seven dance studios within the greater Monroe Township. Elizabeth Bianchi knew every dance troupe and every dancer. More importantly, Elizabeth knew every community representative judging that day's competition.

Elizabeth parked the car. Peggy reached for the handle to make her exit. "Be careful, baby." Elizabeth beckoned Peggy. "I don't want you to trip and sprain an ankle." Peggy was thrilled to see the other children; many she'd come to know through dance.

"Pauline, grab your sister's costumes, and be careful! I'll get the brownies."

Pauline carefully lifted the costumes that had been sitting next to her in the backseat. She would have to come back to retrieve Peggy's Carryall. She walked a few feet behind her mother, avoiding any potentially embarrassing criticism her mother might have for her. Such would not be the case this morning. Elizabeth adorned herself with the most gracious of her numerous personalities.

"Grace! Good morning, dear," Elizabeth greeted Grace Paring. "Is Daniella ready for today?" Grace Paring knew Elizabeth Bianchi all too well and tried her best to not allow the conversation to continue past a casual greeting.

"Good morning, Liz. I think Daniella is ready. She's been practicing every day. I hope all the kids have a good time today," Grace politely responded as she gently pushed Daniella ahead.

Elizabeth moved closer to Daniella. "Would you like a brownie?"

Grace smiled knowingly as she gently pushed the tray from her daughter. "Thank you, Liz. I don't want Daniella getting chocolate on her costume."

Elizabeth laughed. "Oh, my goodness. I didn't even think of that!" Turning back to Daniella, she asked, "Are you scared? There are going to be a lot of people watching."

Grace abruptly took Daniella's shoulders and turned her away from Elizabeth. "Thank you, Elizabeth. I hope Peggy does well this morning."

Elizabeth smiled, "Oh, she will, Grace; she will do very well."

Elizabeth and Peggy walked to the contestant's registration booth. Pauline, lagging, walked over to Daniella. "I know you'll do well, Daniella," Pauline encouraged.

Grace, still furious with Elizabeth's undermining, took Daniella's hand.

"Come along, Daniella. We don't need more encouragement from the Bianchis!"

Pauline stood alone with costumes in hand, wondering if she'd once again said something inappropriate.

"Pauline! Get over here! Your sister needs to get ready." Pauline rushed to her mother's side. "Pauline, this is a very important day for Peggy. Just be quiet and do as you are told," Elizabeth instructed. "Where is your sister's Carryall?"

Frustrated with the entire morning, Pauline shouted, "I couldn't hold everything!"

Elizabeth retorted, "You watch the way you speak to your mother, young lady! If I wasn't holding these brownies, I'd..."

At that moment, Mr. James Kimble walked through the door. Elizabeth instantaneously transformed into miss congeniality. "Oh, Mr. Kimble. We were just looking for you," Elizabeth gushed.

James Kimble was the event organizer. He'd been a contributor to Jonesby Dance Academy since its inception in 1946. Mr. Kimble owned and operated Kimble Distribution, a produce distribution center, providing fresh produce throughout Monroe Township.

"Would you like a deep, dark chocolate brownie?" Elizabeth tempted.

"Well, thank you..." he paused, momentarily forgetting her name.

Elizabeth, not wanting to create an awkward moment, interjected, "Elizabeth, Elizabeth Bianchi. And this is our little dancer, Peggy. Say hello to Mr. Kimble, Peggy."

Peggy, still holding her mother's hand, brought her other hand to her mouth and hid behind her mother. Elizabeth explained, "She's just a little shy this morning. But you just wait till she hits that stage! She will burst out of her shell!"

Mr. Kimble reached for a brownie and chuckled. "I'm sure she will! And who is this pretty young lady?" he asked, turning his attention to Pauline.

"Oh, that's Peggy's sister. Come along, Pauline, we've got to get your sister ready."

"Won't you be dancing, Pauline?" Mr. Kimble asked.

Elizabeth threw her head back with a laugh. "Oh my goodness, no! Peggy is the dancer in the family. Come along, Pauline. I'm sure Mr. Kimble has things he has to attend do." Pauline walked a few steps in front of her mother and sister. Elizabeth turned her attention back to Mr. Kimble. "I do hope the brownie is all right. They should still be slightly warm."

Mr. Kimble took a bite. "Oh, my Lord! I just might have to take another for later." He took a napkin and reached for a second brownie. "These are simply sinful! Thank you, Mrs. Bianchi. I look forward to seeing our little Miss Peggy's numbers!"

Elizabeth feigned a blush. "Thank you, Mr. Kimble." Elizabeth looked from side to side, making certain no one was watching. Placing her hand gently on Mr. Kimble's lapel, she whispered, "If you want another brownie, Mr. Kimble, they will be in the judges' room."

Mr. Kimble whispered in response, "Thank you, my dear."

Elizabeth smiled, *one down.*

CHAPTER EIGHT

I'M ALL EARS

"So, you're telling me Pauline's mother was just as manipulative and evil as Pauline?" I asked, not quite as shocked as my voice hinted.

"No, Mr. Dustin. I am simply telling you what I have heard from the people I have talked to. Their stories all corroborated. Elizabeth had a Jekyll and Hyde personality."

"Perhaps your description is better than ours was. We knew Pauline as 'Old Sweet & Sour.'"

He politely smiled, but it quickly vanished as he continued. "There was a very dark period for the Bianchi family. Families tend to go through periods like that, ya know. They are defining periods where unintended decisions can be made that last a lifetime."

"Okay. I'm all ears." *I know you are going to tell me about it anyway,* I thought to myself.

CHAPTER NINE
LIFE CHANGES
SEPTEMBER 1958

It had been six years since the Bianchis received the letter. Six years since the 2nd Division Infantry was ordered to the front line to relieve the 45th Infantry Division on Old Baldy Hill. If that order had never occurred, Douglas Bianchi would have returned home one month later. Instead, the Bianchis received the letter informing them of Private First-Class Douglas Franklin Bianchi's death.

Pauline relived the moment every time she walked past her brother's room. It had become a shrine. Everything was exactly as he'd left it six years earlier. It looked as if it was awaiting his home-coming—a homecoming that was never to take place.

Pauline's mother suffered from the loss of her son but found solace in the attention she gained as a result of his death. Families rallied around her, supported her, and honored her for her son's ulti-mate sacrifice. Pauline was repulsed by her mother's manipulation of her friends' sympathies. In Pauline's mind, Douglas's death was her mother's convenient means of pirating the recognition he'd earned with his life.

Peggy, now thirteen, was too young and too busy with other

things to have developed a close connection with her older brother. His death was a horrible loss, but it was yesterday's loss—not to be revisited daily. However, her relationship with Pauline strengthened as their mother's demands on Peggy increased. Peggy had realized Elizabeth's love was conditional. Perform well, give a reason for her boastful excesses, and Peggy would be rewarded with affection. Falter—cause her mother to be embarrassed—and she too would be the recipient of the woman's scorn.

Pauline was fifteen years of age. Elizabeth made every attempt to drive a wedge between the two. By this time, belittling Pauline in front of Peggy served to deepen the already calloused emotions Pauline had toward her mother. Although it troubled Peggy to witness her mother's brutality directed at her older sister, Peggy followed Pauline's advice and did not get involved. Time would offer them opportunities to strengthen their bond.

Frank Bianchi never spoke of the loss of his son. Douglas represented hope. He represented the continuation of the Bianchi name. Frank saw a great deal of himself in Douglas. After receiving news of his son's sacrifice, Frank, Pauline's white knight, died on the battlefield with his son.

There were no further arguments between Frank and Elizabeth. He seemed completely unfazed by her relentless badgering, giving only a slight smile and retreating into his unknown, unseen world of silent despondency.

CHAPTER TEN
TEEN YEARS
APRIL 9, 1959

Paige Cervoni was the first to cast an eye on him. Paige, Pauline's closest friend, was always the first to notice any new boy in the neighborhood.

Her hands shook, and she could barely dial Pauline's telephone number.

"Mrs. Bianchi? Mrs. Bianchi? This is Paige. Is Pauline there? I need to talk to her!"

"She's here somewhere," Elizabeth replied. The boredom in her voice was evident. "Pauline. Pauline, Paige is on the telephone —again!"

"Tell her I'll be right down, Mother," Pauline replied.

"I'm not your servant! Get down here and take your call, and don't be on long!"

Pauline scampered down the stairs and took the receiver from her mother. "What's your tale, nightingale?"

"Pauline! I'm about to flip! The dreamiest guy just moved in! Pauline, I think I've seen my future husband!" Paige gushed.

"And I suppose you're calling to ask me to be your maid of honor?" Pauline scoffed.

"Pauline, no kidding. He is the most!"

"Well, what's his name? What does he look like? How old is he?" Pauline asked.

"What? Are you writing a book? I don't have all the specifics yet; wait till you see him!" Paige squealed.

"Pauline, get off the phone!" Elizabeth shouted.

"Mom, I just got on the phone!" Pauline shouted back.

"Did you hear me? Off!"

"Paige, I've got to split. My mother is having another one of her hissy fits."

"That's okay, Paul. I just had to call and clue you in. I'll see you tomorrow."

The Romano family moved in across the street and two doors down from the Cervonis. Paige's upstairs bedroom faced the street—the perfect roost for Paige to observe her new neighbor's comings and goings. She did her best to hide any sunlight reflection from the lenses of her binoculars while ever so slightly separating the Venetian blinds to peer through.

There were three children in the new family. A young boy, Paige estimated him to be eight or nine years old, and a younger girl—perhaps five. Then, there was her future husband, the father of her children, the tall, dark, and handsome man of her dreams!

"Mamma. We should bake a pie for the new neighbors. It's the Christian thing to do."

"What's he look like, Paige?" her mother knowingly asked.

"Oh, Mother!" Paige sounded incredulous—she then began to giggle. "He's a dream!"

"Uh-huh; thought so!" Paige's mother joined her giggles. "All right, sweetheart. We'll bake a pie for them." She paused for a moment. "I don't suppose I could get you to take it over to them, could I?"

"Ooooooh, Mother! Stop talking and start baking!" Paige demanded in mocking desperation.

Three hours later, the fragrance of freshly baked apple pie wafted through the Cervoni home.

"Paige? Paige!" Mrs. Cervoni called. "You've been in front of that mirror for over an hour. I thought *we* were going to bake the pie."

"I was the one who came up with the idea, Momma; and I'm the one who has to deliver it," Paige called back.

Dolly Cervoni just smiled and shook her head, remembering her own teen years. It was, after all, one of her freshly baked pies that won the heart of Paige's father.

Dolly removed her apron and walked down the hall to the bedroom. She wanted to freshen up a bit just in case the new neighbors decided to drop by to introduce themselves.

"Honey, I'm home!" Robert, Paige's father, announced as he entered.

"Hi, Daddy! I've got exciting news for you," Paige called from the upstairs bathroom.

"I can't wait to hear it," her father called back.

The aroma of freshly baked hot apple pie captured Robert's memories like a siren song. What better way to show his appreciation than to cut just a sliver and be gleefully gorging himself as his wife and daughter walked into the kitchen to greet him?

"DADDY NO! WHAT HAVE YOU DONE?" Paige shrieked in horror.

"Robert honey, that was meant for the new neighbors across the street."

"YOU'VE RUINED EVERYTHING! EVERYTHING! MY LIFE IS RUINED!" Paige ran up the stairs in tears. Her bedroom door slammed behind her.

Robert stood in shock. Adhered to his lips, a crumb let go and tumbled onto the floor. "What the heck did I do?"

"Honey, you fathered a little girl who has now become a teenager. Life as you once knew it will never be the same." Dolly gently wiped the corner of his mouth. "Dinner will be a little late. I have another apple pie to bake."

Dolly climbed the stairs and knocked on Paige's door. "Paige honey. Let's make another apple pie. It will be even better." Dolly waited. No response. "I promise this one will be perfect!"

The door slowly opened. "I didn't mean to be so angry with Daddy, Momma. Is he mad at me?" Paige asked.

"Honey, no. He didn't know, and freshly baked apple pie is his Achilles heel. Come on down and let's get something to eat before it's too late. You can still make your *special delivery*!"

The second pie was perfect. Robert jokingly volunteered to taste it—just to make certain it met his high standards. Paige was not amused.

"On second thought, I'll just enjoy the first pie," he said.

Paige hugged him. All was forgiven—all was at peace. Paige made her way to the new neighbor's home. She was suddenly struck by the possibility her future husband might not be the one answering the door—what then? What if his mother or father answered the door?

What would she say? *Hi, I'm Paige Cervoni. I live right over there and our family wanted to welcome you to the neighborhood... WHERE'S YOUR SON?* No, that wouldn't work. *Hello. I'm Paige Cervoni. Welcome to the neighborhood. Do you have any children—my age?* Still awkward.

She was oblivious to the fact that as she continued to rehearse numerous failed lines—she was getting closer to her destination! Her senses returned to her as she found herself pushing the doorbell. She heard footsteps; the door opened.

"Hi."

She forgot to plan for the possibility that HE would answer the door.

"Uh, hi. I'm Paige. Did you just move in? I... I mean. I know you just moved in; obviously, you just moved in. I... I brought you an apple pie. Do you like apple pie?" As hard as Paige tried, she could not stop her lips from moving and the words from pouring out. "I'm glad you live here. I mean, my family wants to welcome you... not just you, but your family. I mean... I mean, they want to welcome you too, but... Oh darn! Hi. I'm Paige." She was flustered, humiliated, and exhausted.

"Hi, Paige. I'm Marc; well, Joshua-Marc, but I prefer to go by Marc. You can call me Marc," the young man calmly said.

"Hi. I'm Paige—you can call me..." she paused, realizing she'd stuttered into an embarrassing corner, "Paige."

"Paige it is! It's a pleasure to meet you." Marc was polite, calm, and reassuring—a true gentleman. "Which house do you live in?" he asked.

"I live right over there." Paige nodded toward her home. "The one with the green Chevy in the driveway."

"Cool. It's nice to meet you, neighbor." Marc waited for a response, any response.

Paige stood on the top step, holding the pie with both hands, nervously rocking back and forth. "Okay, well, cool. Good to meet you, Marc. I hope to see you around." Her outburst was uncomfortably abrupt. As she turned to walk away, Marc's voice stopped her mid-step.

"Uh, Paige?"

Paige nervously turned around. "Yes?"

"I'm sorry, but did you... did you want to leave the pie?" Marc awkwardly asked.

Paige looked down. Somehow, her hands still had a death grip on the pie tin that held the perfect apple pie she'd meant to deliver. "Oh, my goodness! Yes, yes. I wanted to leave the pie; of course, I want to leave the pie! How silly of me; the pie!" Paige couldn't stop babbling. "I'm sorry. I'm--I'm really sorry." Paige repeated as she walked back up the porch steps. She desperately needed reassurance. "Marc? Was this a good first meeting?" she asked clumsily.

Marc chuckled. "Paige, I think this was a very good first meeting. Thank you for the pie. I look forward to seeing you again." It was just the reassurance Paige needed.

Paige released the security of the pie into Marc's hands. She slowly turned and walked away. *I look forward to seeing you again.* His words repeated in her head. Her tempo increased as she stepped off the curb and onto the street. *I look forward to seeing you again!* By the time she reached her front door, she was in a full sprint. *I look forward to seeing you again!* Her father opened the screen door as Paige flung herself into his arms. "He's the one, Daddy! He's the one!"

A confused Robert asked, "The one who, what? Who is HE?"

Dolly walked up behind Robert while Paige was still hugging him. She lovingly patted him on the shoulder and whispered, "Never mind, sweetheart. Just hug your daughter."

The next morning, at seven o'clock, the telephone rang. Elizabeth, shaken from a deep sleep, jumped from her bed and stormed into the kitchen. "*Someone better be dead!*" she grumbled in Italian.

"Good morning, Mrs. Bianchi. It's Paige. Can I talk to Pauline?"

"*It's seven o'clock on a Saturday morning! What's wrong with your mother, letting you call at seven?*" Elizabeth spat into the receiver.

"I'm sorry, Mrs. Bianchi. I don't speak Italian very well," Paige hesitated. "But good morning to you, too. Can I speak to Pauline?"

Elizabeth boiled with rage, "Paolino! *It's that idiot friend of yours. Tell her not to call before eleven.*"

"I'm coming, I'm coming!" Pauline raced down the stairs and into the kitchen. Elizabeth shoved the telephone receiver into her chest and stormed back into her bedroom.

"Hello?"

"Pauline! Oh, my goodness! Pauline, he's a dream. He is so fab. Talk about a flutter bum..."

"Wait a minute, wait a minute. Who?" Pauline asked.

"Marc silly! Marc, the new boy that moved in across the street!" Paige chided.

"You mean you met him? His name is Marc. You talked with him?"

"Shhhh! Yes, we hung out together last night. I'm really gone! I think he likes me. He said he wants to get together again!" Paige squealed with excitement.

"That's swell, Paige. I'm happy for you." Pauline replied, neither convinced nor convincing.

"Did you invite him to youth group?" Pauline asked.

"Not yet. But I will." Paige took a deep breath. "So, how are you and Jerry doing?"

"Jerry and me? We're friends, that's all; friends."

"Come on, Pauline. Everyone knows you and Jerry are on the hook."

"We are friends, Paige. That's all."

Paige was testing Pauline's patience.

"Ohhhh! Listen to you. Kind of sensitive, aren't we?" Paige teased.

Pauline had enough of the conversation. "I've told you. Jerry and I are just friends," she said. With devilish enthusiasm, she continued, "But I am interested in meeting Marc."

"OH, NO YOU DON'T! I've got dibs on this one!"

"Toodle-oo, girlfriend. I'll see you tomorrow at church. Oh, and make sure you invite Marc," Pauline giggled.

"PAULINE!" Paige shouted into the receiver, but only the dial tone responded.

CHAPTER ELEVEN

FIRST RELIANCE BAPTIST CHURCH

SUNDAY, APRIL 12, 1959

"Good morning, Bob. Wonderful to see you, Tess. Welcome back, Mrs. Armstrong. I'm glad to see you looking so well."

Pastor Alonzo Ricci's welcome was the highlight of every Sunday morning for many. He positioned himself just outside the sanctuary doors to greet every parishioner as they arrived. He would also give a hearty, but purposefully convicting, wave to any Monroe Township citizens who passed by the church's open doors and failed to enter.

Pastor Ricci had been the pastor at First Reliance Baptist Church for six years. It was his second church. It was his first as Senior Pastor since graduating from Augustana College and New Brunswick Theological Seminary.

A-Ric, as he was known at Augustana College, excelled in the sciences. Professors at the college encouraged students to question everything they'd ever been taught. "Dare to ask the hard questions."

He allowed himself time to walk through the halls of the science department. He felt comfortable examining and probing the strict fundamentalist teachings forced upon him by an overly zealous, pastor-father and overly submissive, angelic mother. The science department was his haven, where creation screamed at him to open his mind and heart to possibilities that otherwise conflicted with his strict upbringing.

As a young man, A-Ric wrestled with the creation story. Because of this struggle, he quietly questioned every other doctrine he'd been taught. Logic told him to move beyond dogma and explore the Bible further through the tangible revelation of archaeological, anthropological, and sociological events hidden under the sands and in the crevices of the mountains. After all, God made all of these, too. His quest was often misunderstood. Such thinking was a threat to his father. However, A-Ric believed scientific findings, locked away in time capsules, awaiting discovery by a later generation—perhaps his generation—could serve to further prove the scriptures. He didn't disbelieve; he didn't doubt—he simply didn't know.

It was an honest search for truth. He meant no disrespect for the scriptures as they were taught to him. A-Ric had a profound desire to know them more experientially and to apply them in a more contemporary manner.

When the Ricci family first arrived in Monroe Township, Pastor Al (as he was known throughout the township) made it a point to shake the hands of every individual in the community. With the determination of a politician walking his precinct, Pastor Al met every person, knew every need and, ultimately, every secret. He was deeply in tune with every family—except his own.

Like many pastors, Pastor Al replenished his personal need for acceptance by serving others. He quietly hoarded their appreciative accolades while outwardly expressing a humble spirit. He secretly wrestled with his unquenchable need for approval. He loved his wife and son—but his family would wait—they had to wait. He rationalized the imbalance of tangible love and attention for them as the downside. It was the necessary sacrifice and consequence of his ministerial calling.

"Hello and welcome to First Reliance. I'm Pastor Ricci. I don't believe we've met." Pastor Ricci reached out his hand. It was met with a firm grip and a warm smile from Marcello Romano.

"Hello, Pastor Ricci. No, we haven't. We just moved into the neighborhood. My name is Marcello Romano. This is my wife Cecilia and our children, Edward, Julietta, and Joshua-Marc."

Joshua-Marc reached out his hand. "My friends all call me Marc."

"Well then, I'd like to call you Marc!" Pastor Ricci said as he shook Marc's hand. "I trust we will become friends!" He turned his attention back to Marcello and Cecilia. "I am so happy you folks are here this morning. Consider yourselves my guests!"

The Romanos entered the foyer of the church. Irene McCarthy played the organ as the chatter of friends greeting friends mingled with the background of her uplifting music.

Marc entered the sanctuary slowly, deliberately. He purposefully observed the congregation of parishioners. He watched how they greeted one another, how they were dressed, and where they sat. He looked to his left—down the back row of young teens. Paige and Pauline sat with Mike D'Amato, Tyler Isom, Danny DeSoto, Trina Hawthorne, and Jerry Pennypacker.

Pauline was first to look up and see Marc; she gasped and gripped Jerry's hand. Jerry, thinking his prayers had been answered, gently, gratefully squeezed Pauline's hand. Marc's smile captured her attention. Marc turned and walked up the aisle with his family. Pauline suddenly realized she was holding Jerry Pennypacker's hand.

"Jerold Pennypacker!" Pauline scolded as she slapped his arm. "What do you think you are doing?"

"I was just... I... Pauline—YOU TOOK MY HAND!" a confused Jerry responded.

"I did nothing of the sort. Shame on you—and in church!" Pauline hoped the new visitor did not see Jerry's inappropriate advances.

"But..." Jerry stopped himself before continuing. With a shrug of his shoulders, he relinquished Pauline's hand.

"Pauline! Pauline! That's him, that's Marc! That's my future husband!" Paige's exuberant whispers were anything but quiet. Betty Bain, seated two rows in front of them, turned and glared her disapproval.

Ignoring Mrs. Bain, Paige continued, "Isn't he a dream?"

Pauline watched as the young man and his family walked to the front of the sanctuary. He politely let his mother, father, and siblings enter the pew before taking his position on the end closest to the center aisle. As he sat, Pauline detected an ever so slight glance in her direction.

"He's a flutter bum all right, a real flutter bum, Paige," Pauline acknowledged, while still looking at the seated visitor.

John Hutto stepped to the podium, cueing Irene to increase the volume of the organ and segue into the last three bars of "Holy, Holy, Holy." The chatter immediately ended as the entire congregation joyfully began singing.

> Holy, holy, holy
> Lord God almighty
> Early in the morning, my song shall rise to thee
> Holy, holy, holy
> Merciful and mighty
> God in three persons, blessed Trinity.

Pastor Ricci shouted, "Amen and amen," as he stepped onto the podium. John Hutto stepped to the side and Pastor Ricci took his place at the lectern.

"Good morning to each one of you! A very special welcome to our guests this morning. We'd like to get to know you better, so if you'd fill out our special guest card and place it on the communion plate when the offering is taken, we'll make sure to greet you in a more personal way!"

Pastor Ricci gave John a friendly pat on the back, "John, get back up here and lead us in a song of celebration!"

John Hutto returned to the microphone. "Take your hymnals and turn with me to Hymn number forty-one, 'To God Be the Glory!'"

It was a polished performance; their routine was impeccable. Sunday after Sunday it was the same but without a sense of boring repetition. The call to worship, the welcome, and the opening celebratory hymn told the congregation, within these walls, there is peace, safety, and harmony.

To make any alterations in the anticipated opening would be thought of as heresy. Irene played the last four bars of "To God Be the Glory" which allowed ample time for the congregation to turn to page forty-one and begin singing.

The music reached a crescendo for the next two songs. Following the offering, the music began to decrescendo in intensity as John Hutto prepared the congregation for Pastor Ricci's message.

Pastor Ricci returned to the podium. "Thank you, my brother, for preparing our hearts for God's word." He then turned his attention to the congregation. "Take your Bibles and turn with me to the thirteenth chapter of the first book of Corinthians. We will be focusing our attention on verses four through seven. If you don't have a Bible, feel free to use one of the Bibles provided in the back of the pew in front of you." He paused while the pages turned. "Let us pray."

"Dear God, open our eyes to what you would have us see in your word. Purge our hearts so that they may become pure vessels suitable to carry that word to a world in need. Amen." The congregation repeated in unison, "Amen."

"Today we are going to focus our attention on what God has to say to us about love."

Paige was ecstatic. Pastor Ricci's very first statement was, in her mind, a confirmation from God about her future with Marc. For Pauline, the music was over, and a very long commercial was about to begin.

As in every church service, Pauline forced her attention to wander. Having taken a three-inch green pencil from the back of the pew in front of her, she meticulously filled in every letter on the guest card. She counted the number of women in the congregation wearing head coverings. Depending upon the length of the sermon, Pauline would intensify her census, determining the inventory of pillbox hats, headband caps with netting, skull caps, and berets—anything to divert her attention from the message. The length of today's sermon allowed Pauline to complete her survey and privately select the winning parishioner's headwear. It was without a doubt Mrs. Lukins, wearing a very stylish Juliette pheasant feather matador hat.

Pauline's private awards ceremony was interrupted as the congregation stood to the familiar sound of the choir singing, "Just as I Am." She'd made it through another service unscathed by Pastor Ricci's menacing ministerial attack.

The congregation closed the service in song. This gave Pastor Ricci and Anna, his wife, time to make their way to the back of the church to shake hands with everyone in attendance.

> Blessed be the tie that binds
> our hearts in Christian love;
> the fellowship of kindred minds
> is like to that above.

Alonzo, in the first row of the church, stood and gave a wave to his youth group, who were seated in the back. Stepping into the center aisle, he met the Romano family for the first time.

"Welcome to First Reliance. My name is Alonzo Ricci. I am the youth director here. This is your first time here, isn't it?"

"Yes, this is our first time. My name is Marcello Romano. This is my wife Cecilia and our children, Edward, Julietta, and Joshua-Marc," Mr. Romano said while shaking Alonzo's outstretched hand.

"It's a pleasure to meet each one of you. Joshua-Marc, if you have a second, I'd like to introduce you to our youth group."

"Go ahead and meet the others, Joshua," Marcello encouraged his son.

Alonzo smiled and led the way through the crowds who were emptying into the center aisle. Like his father, Alonzo shook hands and exchanged pleasantries as he made his way to the back of the church.

"My friends call me Marc," Marc coyly mentioned as they neared the last rows.

Alonzo stopped. "What was that?"

"My name; my friends call me Marc. I'd like to be called Marc."

"Well then, Marc it is! Hey, gang. I've got a new friend to introduce to you. This is my friend Marc Romano. Marc, this is the greatest youth group in all of Monroe Township!"

Alonzo continued, "Hey, Marc. We get together every Sunday night for our youth meeting at six o'clock, and then we go out for ice cream at Bray's after the evening service. I hope you can join us tonight. It'll give you a chance to meet everyone."

Marc immediately looked at Paige. "I've met some already." Paige blushed, shyly looked away, and then back at Marc, but Marc's gaze moved to Pauline. "But I haven't met everyone yet." Pauline smiled; her eyes did not stray from his.

CHAPTER TWELVE
DAMNED
SUNDAY, APRIL 12, 1959

The Romano family made their way to the back of the church where Alonzo was introducing Marc to the youth group.

"Mr. Romano, allow me to introduce you to our youth group," Alonzo offered.

"It's a pleasure to meet you," Mr. Romano replied. "Joshua, let's get going. Your mother has stew in the crockpot."

Marc shook hands with Alonzo. "It was nice to meet you, Alonzo." He turned to the youth group. "Great meeting everyone. I'm sure I'll see you again."

Paige eagerly interrupted, "Maybe for ice cream tonight?"

Mr. Romano chuckled. "We'll see." He turned his attention back to Alonzo. "We're visiting a few of the churches in the area. I must say, I enjoyed your service this morning. Thank you for your hospitality."

"Mr. Romano, you, and your family are never visitors here. You are guests! Thanks for joining us. I hope we see you again soon."

Everyone filed out the sanctuary doors. Everyone except Pauline.

Avoiding Pastor Ricci was her primary goal. Pauline separated herself from the group and made her way to the side door.

She knew she was damned; she had to be. Every one of Pastor Al's left her with the impression they were directed at her. As much as she tried to hide her self-incriminating heart, he somehow knew its darkness and would unforgivingly expose her before the entire congregation. Oh, he would never call her by name—but he was preaching at her—she knew it; she could feel it.

Her emotions, her thoughts, and her feelings condemned her. She considered her hopelessness *fait accompli*. Condemned to be one of the unlucky ones, she would remain lost, incapable of saving grace, unchosen—even by God.

"It is so unfair," she thought. *"I don't want to go to hell. I don't want to be damned forever. Why can't I be chosen? How can a loving God condemn someone who is already condemning themselves?"*

Pauline found herself wrestling with these questions every Sunday morning during Pastor Al's messages. It was the reason she counted the slats in the ceiling, lightbulbs in the fixtures, and the number of bubbles in the communion cups as they passed by on the first Sunday of every month. It was how she noticed the many times Mrs. Wilkerson, who was seated center stage in the choir, would nod her head and give her smarmy smile in showy approval of Pastor Al's message. She would do anything to avoid focusing on the convicting words of Pastor Al's messages and Pastor Al.

"Hey, Pauline. Pauline!" Alonzo's call shot a shiver up Pauline's spine. "Hey, I'm glad I caught you. Is there any chance we can get together before the youth group meeting tonight?"

Alonzo's invitation left Pauline with a sick hollow feeling in the pit of her stomach. Did he know? Had his father mentioned her? She'd tried to be inconspicuous—blend in with the rest of the youth group. Why would he want to talk to her?

"Uh, well sure. Sure, I guess. Let me ask my mom."

"Ask your mother what, sweetheart?" Elizabeth asked as she came up from behind Pauline.

"Good morning, Alonzo. Please let the pastor know how much we enjoyed his message," Elizabeth gushed.

"I'll certainly let him know, Mrs. Bianchi. Pauline and I were just talking about the possibility of getting together before the youth meeting tonight—say, about five o'clock?"

Elizabeth stroked Pauline's hair as she responded to Alonzo. "Why certainly, Alonzo. I'll make certain she is here promptly."

"Ah, that will be great." Alonzo turned his attention to Pauline. "I'll see you then."

As they walked back to the car, Elizabeth tightly grabbed Pauline's arm. "What have you done now?"

"I've done nothing, Mother. You're hurting me." Pauline pulled away and entered the car.

Elizabeth dropped Pauline off at 4:50 pm. Pauline took note of Alonzo's car parked in the adjacent parsonage. It was a beautiful red 1957 Chevy Bel Air Matador with a black and red cloth interior. Alonzo kept it sparkling. Pauline's stomach churned as she exited her mother's car.

"You listen to me, young lady! I want you to watch what you do and what you say. I've worked hard to be highly respected here, and I do not want you to ruin it for the family by acting inappropriately!"

Pauline continued her exit, placing one foot on the asphalt.

Her mother continued, "You are meeting with the pastor's son! I don't know what you've done, but I will not have you dragging the Bianchi name in the mud. You just sit there, listen—and apologize for whatever you've done! Do you hear me?"

Pauline stepped out of the car and closed the door. She could hear the muffled shouts of her mother, "Pauline Bianchi, I asked you a question! Do you hear me?" Pauline turned and walked toward the hall leading to the youth room and Alonzo's office.

She reached for the doorknob only to have it slip from her grasp as the door opened.

"Pauline! You are right on time. Come in, come in! Golly, I am glad you were able to meet with me. I've been wanting to get together, but the time just never presented itself. How are you?"

How am I? I'm sick to my stomach and about to puke; that's how I am! Pauline quietly thought.

"I'm fine Alonzo. How has your day been?"

"Ha! It's Sunday. Sundays are always busy for me. If I don't look overworked and harried by two o'clock, my father finds multiple things for me to do!" Alonzo replied.

Alonzo held his office door open for Pauline. "Grab a seat on that old leather couch over there and make yourself comfortable. I think it was made from the hide of one of the cows that came off Noah's ark."

Pauline chuckled, "It is a bit worn."

"Worn? Are you kidding me? It was *a bit worn* fifty years ago." Once again, they both laughed. Pauline was beginning to feel at ease.

Alonzo left the door open and sat down across from Pauline. "So, tell me; who is Pauline Bianchi?"

The question caught Pauline off guard. "Excuse me?" Pauline nervously responded.

Alonzo, with absolute poise and professionalism, repeated his question. "Who is this young lady sitting in my office, who attends every youth activity, who is at every church service, and is somehow capable of remaining mysteriously hidden within the group? I want to get to know you, and it just seems to me the best person to ask about you would be," Alonzo paused, and with piercing blue eyes Pauline had never before noticed said, "you."

"Golly, Alonzo. I'm nobody special. I just come to church. I know the kids in the group, and I like getting together with them." She paused and abruptly said, "Oh, and you, too."

Alonzo laughed. "Oh, sure. I bet I'm a big reason you come."

Pauline was feeling surprisingly comfortable with their conversation. "No, really Alonzo. I like you. I don't know." She paused to gather her thoughts. "Your dad is great and all, but I think he's got something against me." Pauline waited to see if Alonzo would respond with an inquiry. He did not. "He always preaches at me—ya know?"

Alonzo sat back in his chair. "Pauline, I know all too well. I get his messages Sunday, Monday, Tuesday, Wednesday." He'd made his point but continued, "Pauline, I'm preached at every day of the week." Alonzo sat forward in his chair and his eyes softened with empathy. "I understand. Pauline, none of us are perfect. My dad always tells me, 'None of us are perfect,' but none of us should relax in being imperfect either!"

Pauline was puzzled. "What does that mean?"

"I think he is trying to say we should always strive to be better and not just settle with our imperfections as if we have no responsibility for them," Alonzo replied.

"Oh, I'm responsible," Pauline lamented. "I'm responsible for everything—ask my mother."

Alonzo didn't pry, but he didn't remove his eyes from Pauline's. The office became uncomfortably quiet. Alonzo and Pauline sat there for a moment without moving. Pauline was the first to speak. "Alonzo, does God choose some people to go to hell?"

Alonzo sat back in his chair. It was a question he must have asked himself over and over again. His father seemed to preach some people were predestined for heaven and some predestined for hell. He wouldn't say it in so many words—no one was really predestined for hell—they just weren't predestined for heaven. The notion must not have set well with Alonzo, because he nervously shifted in his seat before he leaned forward, clasping his hands.

"Pauline, no—I don't believe so. I don't believe so at all. I'll admit, I don't know the mind of God, but I know God is love and I know God forgives." Alonzo took a deep breath and unclasped his hands. "Honestly? I don't know. I mean, I understand the words, but I am not sure any of us can comprehend the sovereignty of God to fully understand the fairness of His election." Alonzo folded his hands just above his chin, just under his mouth. "The way I see it is very simple. Jesus said in John 6:37 whoever comes to the Father, I will in no wise cast out. The Bible says, 'He died for all because all have sinned. For God so loved the world that he gave his only begotten Son.' We know God's word is true so when we experience His conviction, we have a decision to make. We can turn from our ways, believe, and follow His ways, or we can stubbornly refuse, reject, and return to our own way. If we *elect* to turn and follow, He is always faithful to have *elected* to receive us." Satisfied with what he heard himself say he concluded, "Pauline, the important thing is He really loves you."

Pauline sat back in her seat and nervously laughed. Alonzo flinched and his eyes widened. "No, really. God loves you!" Alonzo paused. "I just wanted to get together and let you know that I am genuinely grateful for your faithfulness. You may not be a magpie, but I am really glad you are part of the youth group."

"I'm sorry, Alonzo. I don't mean to be quiet. I don't mean to be standoffish. I like the youth group; I like it a lot." Pauline inhaled and let it out slowly. "My mother made me go to church when I was younger—I hated it. She would parade my sister and tell me to behave. She'd say 'Don't embarrass me!'" Pauline sat up straight as if she's just received enlightening news. "I don't like her, Alonzo. I don't like my mother at all." Pauline looked down at her folded hands now resting in her lap. "Is that terribly wrong?" Pauline raised her head once again. "Alonzo, you see her at church, but you don't know…"

"Pauline, don't be so hard on yourself. My goodness, girl! You've got to give yourself a break. We all love you and want you to feel at home in the youth group. You speak when you want to speak and be quiet when you want to be quiet. I want you to know my door is always open."

Pauline returned her gaze to her folded hands. "Thank you. Thank you very much, Alonzo."

CHAPTER THIRTEEN
ICE-CREAM SOCIAL
SUNDAY, APRIL 12, 1959

"No. NO JERRY!" Pauline firmly scolded.

"Pauline, we've been kinda seeing each other for three months. What do you have against a kiss?" a dejected Jerry asked.

"In the church parking lot? Really? Jerry, you are a dear friend. I like you—I like you a lot, but I don't have those kinds of feelings for you—not yet. Can't we enjoy being best friends?" Pauline innocently asked.

Jerry removed his cramped right arm that was awkwardly wedged between Pauline's neck and the headrest. "Oh, sure. Sure, we can," he mockingly responded. "Just like brother and sister—great."

"Jerold Pennypacker! If that is all you are looking for..." Pauline did not complete her assumptive accusation.

"Pauline, you know me better than that. I respect you. I just thought it might be time for us to, you know, take the next step in our..." he paused, "... in our relationship."

Pauline abruptly turned away from Jerry and stared out the windshield. "It's not the next step I am worried about Jerold Pennypacker. It's how long a walk you're intending to take." Pauline locked her arms across her chest.

"Pauline, I didn't want to make you mad. Look, I want to have a good time. I just thought, well, you know. I'm sorry if I came on too strong. You're really pretty, and I sorta like to think of you as my girl. I wasn't trying to pressure you at all. I'm sorry," Jerry humbly apologized.

Pauline was enjoying Jerry's groveling. He was a football and basketball letterman at East Brunswick High School, and the president of the First Reliance Baptist Church Youth Group; he had a 4.0 GPA and was an Honor Society Member who was pursued by every major university on a sports scholarship. He was the dream of every girl on campus. The fact that he was pursuing Pauline and she was playing him like a fiddle made the ruse all the more enjoyable.

"It's okay, Jerry. I understand. I'm just not ready to get serious; not just yet." Pauline turned to face Jerry, who appeared to be taking his frustrations out with a stranglehold on the steering wheel.

He looked at Pauline. "Can I ask you a question?"

"Sure, Jerry. What is it?" Pauline responded.

"Got any idea when you MIGHT start thinking about getting more serious?" Jerry sounded as if he was just kidding.

Pauline intuitively knew he was *kidding on the level*. She playfully slapped Jerry's arm. "Silly! Come on. Let's get to Bray's with the rest of the group. Tell ya what, this one is on me."

Bray's Family Drug Store was the high school hangout. Mr. Bray made the best malts in town. His homemade ice cream and hot fudge made even the most dismal date worthwhile. Jerry parked his dad's 1953 Chevy Coupe and opened Pauline's door. Pauline popped out into the cool night air like a happy springer spaniel. This added salt to Jerry's already wounded heart.

"Thank you, Jerry!" Pauline put Jerry's block sweater over her shoulders. While the kids at Reliance knew they were *just friends*, there was no telling what other girls might be at the fountain on a

Sunday night. Having a boy's block sweater over her shoulders was a *'hands off'* message to potential competition.

"Hi, Jerry, Pauline," Mr. Bray welcomed the two from across the front register.

"Hiya, Mr. Bray," Jerry and Pauline responded.

"Come on in, come on in. Mrs. Bray is back there serving a bunch of you kids. She'll be happy to see you two. The fudge just got off the stove, so it's piping hot." Mr. Bray licked his lips, "And goo-ood."

Jerry and Pauline made their way to the back of the store and were met by Alonzo. "What took you so long?" Alonzo asked.

Jerry's face flushed, and he rubbed the back of his neck.

"They were making out in the church bushes and forgot about the time," Danny Miller jokingly blurted out.

The entire youth group broke into spontaneous laughter. Knowing how well the deacons policed the parking lot after evening church services, such a scenario was the most unlikely possibility anyone could think of.

"Well just as long as you put a couple of bucks in the offering plate!" Alonzo teased, grabbing the back of Jerry's neck and giving him a playful tug. "Come on, gang! Let's get some ice cream!"

The fountain was packed with Reliance kids. Pauline quickly scanned the group. Marc was not there.

"Where have you guys been?" Trina Hawthorne asked.

"We took the scenic route," Jerry responded. "What's everyone ordering?"

"Let's get the Everest!" Mike D'Amato shouted out. "It will be huge tonight!"

Mrs. Bray looked up at the ceiling and shook her head. "Will you kids eat it all? I don't want any of you complaining that it's getting mixed," she warned.

The Everest was a combination of everyone's scoops of ice cream piled high in a stainless-steel mixing bowl. It was then topped with flowing hot chocolate, freshly whipped cream, and sprinkled with Spanish peanuts. The key was to put your order in last, so your favorite ice cream remained on the outside of the mound. It was the Matthew 20:26 rule, *"So the last shall be first and the first last."* Put your order in first and you either have to wait until it becomes exposed, or you have to attempt to excavate through your friend's orders to find it. Either way, when you reached your scoop it would have become an unrecognizable Neapolitan blob!

"Hey, Mrs. Bray. What's the best ice cream today? I want the best," Danny jokingly shouted.

"You're going to have the liver and onion flavor I made just for you, Danny," Mrs. Bray shouted back. Everyone joined in the laughter.

By this time, Alonzo had written the numbers one through twenty-eight on individual pieces of a torn paper napkin and put them in a bowl. All twenty-eight high schoolers reached into the bowl for a number. Danny Miller reached in first and pulled out number one.

"That's it! I'm ordering that liver and onions, and I'm going to eat my way to it!" The entire group broke into laughter.

Mrs. Bray's French vanilla bean was the town's favorite. Most of the kids ordered it. The only other flavors selected were pralines with pecan and, of course, her deep dark chocolate fudge with Spanish nuts.

As the orders were collected, Alonzo whispered to Mrs. Bray, "I think we've got a chance to conquer Everest tonight. I want to thank you and Mr. Bray for your hospitality. The kids and I appreciate it."

Mrs. Bray handed Alonzo a vanilla waffle cone brimming with her deep dark chocolate fudge. "Alonzo, you mean a great deal to these kids and this community. We always look forward to seeing everyone," she smiled, "even David." They both laughed.

CHAPTER FOURTEEN

MIGHT AS WELL ORDER

"So, tell me. Did Pauline stay with Jerry or did she and Marc eventually get together? I mean, it sounds as if there might have been a few sparks flying when they met—right?" I finally interjected, intrigued with the prospect that Pauline had an almost normal adolescence.

He laughed. "I've got ya hooked now, don't I?" He raised his hand as if cautioning me to slow down. "We'll get to that."

It was evident this chat was going to take longer than I expected. At this point, I wanted to hear more. "Why don't we get a bite to eat and you can continue with the story," I asked.

"That sounds great. I understand they've got some pretty good food here at St. Elmo."

We both knowingly laughed. I called our server over to the table. "Hi, what's your name?" I asked our server.

"Hello, Mr. Dustin. My name is Antonio."

"Well, hello, Antonio. It's a pleasure to meet you. Yeah, Bennet usually waits on my family—but it's very nice to meet you."

"I will do everything in my power to equal the service Bennet usually offers, sir." Antonio politely smiled at the two gentlemen and continued. "Let me bring you a couple of menus. Would you like something other than coffee to drink?"

"I'm good with coffee, thanks," my new friend said.

"Ya know, Antonio, I'm good with coffee too. Thank you," I responded.

"Then let me bring you both fresh cups with those menus."

"Okay, you were saying," I urged.

CHAPTER FIFTEEN

MARC'S FIRST YOUTH MEETING
APRIL 1959

The youth trickled in at five forty-five. Twenty-three teens were present until Marc Romano walked into the room.

"Hi, Marc! Welcome to the group!" Paige was unable to contain her enthusiasm. "Let me introduce you to everyone. This is Jerry Pennypacker. He's the best quarterback in Monroe."

Jerry reached out to shake hands with Marc. "Nice to meet you, Marc. You play any sports?"

"Well, yeah." Marc hesitated.

"That's great! What sports?"

"Uh, I play a little football."

"What position?" Jerry continued his questioning.

"Well..." once again Marc appeared hesitant. "I've played, I've played different positions."

"What school? Where did you move from? Play any high school ball?"

Before Marc could respond Danny interrupted. "Wait a minute, wait a minute! I know who you are! You're Joshua Romano! Hey gang, it's Joshua Romano!"

Marc's eyes darted back and forth. Pauline could sense he was looking for an escape.

"Joshua Romano? Why does that name sound familiar?" Jerry asked Danny.

"Are you kidding me? He's only the number one high school quarterback in the five eastern states!" Danny announced, not realizing the implications it might have for Jerry.

Marc and Jerry stared at each other. Marc was the first to speak. "I... I've played other positions too," he apologetically responded.

Paige continued, "And this is Mike. He's the singer in the group and he plays guitar. Tyler wrestles. You met Danny. He is the clown of the group. Trina plays the piano and Pauline..." Paige paused. "Pauline is the quiet one."

Pauline shyly smiled. It was an all too coy expression for Paige to let pass without adding, "She and Jerry hang out together."

Pauline's head immediately swiveled in Paige's direction. The vein in her forehead protruded.

Marc politely addressed the group. "It's nice to meet," he once again fixed his gaze upon Pauline, "all of you."

Paige prompted Marc, "We usually get together for ice cream at Bray's after church."

"Yeah. I'm sorry I missed it last week. It sounds great."

Alonzo entered the room. Seeing Marc he said, "What's buzzin cuzzin?" It was as if Marc had been a member of the group from the beginning. Alonzo was a master at making people feel comfortable. "Alright, you bunch of hipsters, let's get this party rocking!"

Mike adjusted his guitar strap and Trina opened the chorus book. Pauline's assessment of Marc was momentarily interrupted when Paige grabbed her arm.

"Isn't Marc the limit?"

Pauline coldly replied, "Jerry and me?"

Paige oozed innocence. Her unspoken gestures spoke volumes. She tilted her head to the side with her mouth agape and eyes staring aimlessly toward the ceiling. Her shoulders were raised in a defensive posture. She appeared to be naively wondering, *did I say something wrong?*

The disingenuous and somewhat sinister smile Pauline offered Paige in return, was a warning. Pauline was not after Marc—but that could change if Paige wasn't careful.

The meeting went as youth meetings go. The group sang choruses, an offering plate was passed (perhaps practice for later in life since no one ever seemed to contribute), and Alonzo spoke, once again, on maintaining purity in dating relationships. Pauline was certain there had to be other topics in the Bible.

After the evening service, the group made their way to Bray's Pharmacy and had ice cream.

CHAPTER SIXTEEN

DISCIPLESHIP

APRIL 1959

Following the ice-cream social, Alonzo returned to his office. The First Reliance Baptist Church Youth Group was beginning to grow in numbers. It was important that it also experiences spiritual growth. He would spend the remainder of the night, into the early hours of the morning, developing a plan to fulfill this ministerial responsibility.

While Alonzo was proud of the way the group accepted Marc, he was particularly aware of the interest the girls had in their newest member of the group. Such an attraction was *only natural*. It was also *only natural* for contentious jealousies to arise from untamed adolescent emotions. Such potential uprisings could undermine the youth group's cohesiveness.

Alonzo planned to introduce private discipleship meetings with each member of the youth group. While mentoring each individual, Alonzo would listen for signs of contention. The ministry would allow him to stay abreast of his group's attitude and avert an eroding of its overall tranquility.

Pauline was of particular interest. She was quiet, there was no doubt about that. However, Alonzo was impressed by their first meeting. When they'd gotten together, she was very candid about her feelings and spiritual concerns. Pauline's unrestrained honesty held promise. In Pauline Bianchi, Alonzo foresaw hidden leadership —and information.

The telephone call came on Tuesday evening.

Pauline answered, "Hello?"

"Hi, Pauline. It's Alonzo at First Reliance. Is this a good time to call?"

Alonzo's voice summoned that sick feeling in the pit of her stomach. What had she done now? "As good a time as any, I suppose. What's up?

"Great! I wanted to visit with you about a new discipleship program I'm thinking about starting."

Before Alonzo could go further Pauline interrupted. "Alonzo, I'm not the discipleship type, honestly. I just want to go and..." Pauline trailed off. Her mother was in the living room, no doubt listening to everything Pauline was saying. "I can't talk about it right now. I'm really happy with my involvement as it is."

"You listen to your youth director, young lady!" The shout came from the living room. "If he needs you for something, you are available! I'm not going to have it said that my daughter is not cooperating with the leadership of our church," Elizabeth shouted.

Pauline held her hand over the receiver. "Mother! You don't even know what the telephone call is about—AND IT ISN'T ABOUT YOU!"

Pauline returned her attention to Alonzo's call. "I'm sorry, Alonzo. My mother doesn't know when to mind her own business."

"PAULINE!" Elizabeth shouted. "Don't you dare disgrace your mother. Your youth director does not need to have you broadcasting your disrespect."

Alonzo hesitantly interrupted. "Uh, so... this doesn't seem to be a good time, I guess."

"If I am home, it is never a good time, Alonzo," Pauline replied.

"Pauline, look—drop by the church tomorrow any time after school. I'd like to set up a meeting with you," Alonzo offered. "I'd just like you to know what the program is about before you decide whether or not to participate."

"I'll drop by sometime in the afternoon, Alonzo. I don't know what time but if you are there, I'll see you then."

"That sounds like a deal. I'm sorry for disrupting things," Alonzo said.

"Alonzo, trust me. You didn't disrupt a thing. This is how I live."

Pauline hung up the telephone. By the time the receiver touched the cradle, Elizabeth was screaming Italian in Pauline's ear. *"You do whatever you can to embarrass me, Pauline. You and your disrespect."*

Pauline retorted in Italian, "You are the one who does everything possible to embarrass you!" Pauline stormed up the stairs, slamming her bedroom door behind her.

Elizabeth was in hot pursuit. She grabbed the doorknob; it was locked.

"You open this door, young lady. I am not through talking to you!" Elizabeth ordered.

"Oh, now THAT'S where you are wrong, Mother. You ARE through talking to me," Pauline replied.

Pauline confined herself to her room until her father returned. This meant her unsuspecting father would, without warning, walk into an unprovoked battle zone and once again become the recipient of her mother's undeserved wrath.

Several hours later, Pauline heard her father's car pulling into the driveway. Her father exited the car and unlocked the garage door. As he lifted the door up and over his head, he was met by the ranting, raving, and cursing of his wife. Like a weightlifter accomplishing a record press, he no sooner lifted the door than he returned it to its closed position, relocked it, returned to the car, and drove away.

Pauline did not hear him return.

The next morning, Pauline hurried to dress and gathered her books and lunch. She hoped to make her way to school without being noticed.

"Good morning, dear. I've made some eggs and toast this morning," her cloying mother oozed.

Without emotion, Pauline retrieved her lunch from the refrigerator, walked past her mother to the back door, and disingenuously responded, "Enjoy!"

"You just wait till you get home, young lady; you just wait!" Elizabeth yelled.

Without turning to respond, Pauline held one hand up in the air, waved, and yelled back, "Can't wait!"

CHAPTER SEVENTEEN
I'M NOT A DISCIPLE
APRIL 1959

Throughout the day, Pauline could not free herself from the expectation of her meeting with Alonzo—more drama, more pressure, more guilt trips, and more manipulations. Pauline longed for the day she could rid herself of Jamesburg and everything in Monroe Township.

As usual, Alonzo's door was wide open when she arrived.

"Hi, Alonzo," Pauline said as she stood in the open doorway.

"Pauline! What's cook'n good-look'n? Come on in," Alonzo invited. "Take a seat on Ol' Angus." Alonzo laughed at his own joke as he continued. "I decided to name that beast of a couch after our first visit."

Pauline couldn't help but laugh. "Thanks, Alonzo."

"So how was your day? What classes are you taking?" Alonzo asked.

Just as Pauline expected—tertiary conversation, then go in for the kill! "My day was fine."

"And your classes? What classes are you taking?" Alonzo probed.

"I don't particularly know. I sleep through most of them."

Alonzo laughed, "A girl after my own heart! I made it through high school—but I think it was because the faculty couldn't tolerate the idea of putting up with me any longer."

Once again, Pauline found herself joining in the laughter. Alonzo seemed to be genuine. He wasn't the least bit affected by Pauline's aloof attitude.

"My classes are all right. I'm not particularly interested in any one subject." Pauline thought for a moment. "I'm pretty good with numbers. Maybe I'll be a banker someday." She shook her head. "What a dreadful job, counting other people's money."

Alonzo laughed, "Well then. You should try the ministry! There's no money to count—not even your own!" Again, there was brief laughter.

"Pauline, the reason I invited you to come over today is to talk with you about the cohesiveness of our group. As we grow and new people join us, it is important to have a central mission we all can embrace."

"You mean discipleship?" Pauline asked.

"Well, yes. Yes, certainly discipleship. There is also a need to be open with one another and transparent. At some point in our lives, we have to take risks and trust one another, create an impenetrable bond."

Pauline interrupted, "Isn't that a lot to ask? I mean, sorry for being so blunt, but there are people just looking for a victim who is trusting."

"You mean in our group?" a shocked Alonzo inquired.

"In life," Pauline responded. She wondered who the counselor was and who the student was.

"We're all friends, Alonzo. Just let someone outside of our group try to say something about one of us or do something to one of us, and they'll have our entire youth group to answer to. But, that doesn't mean we don't have our own..." Pauline carefully considered her words. "... our family problems here within the group."

Alonzo cleared his throat before responding, "Like what? Can you say? I mean, can you say without betraying someone's confidence?"

Alonzo did not let Pauline respond. Instead, he wanted to further relieve any burden Pauline might feel for being so open. "Listen, I do not want to pry. If things are going on that, you know, normal stuff, high school stuff, guy—gal stuff, you know, stuff that won't hurt the group, I don't need to know all of that. That kind of thing borders on *gospel gossip*. But if things are going on that could shake our cohesiveness, I hope you will trust me enough to let me know. I will never betray your trust and will be there for you when you need me."

The phrase caught Pauline's attention: "*gospel gossip*."

"Oh, yeah. I made that one up!" Alonzo proudly exclaimed. "It's when believers get together and *'share'* about others... seemingly out of love and concern... but everyone knows it is just plain old fashion gossip!"

So, this is discipleship, Pauline thought to herself. "If anything like that was going on I would let you know. Is that all you wanted to talk to me about?" Pauline asked.

"No, no not at all. That doesn't even approach what I want to talk to you and all the guys and gals about," Alonzo explained. "I want to visit with each one individually, weekly—if possible, to encourage and support each person in the group. Whether it's a spiritual need, a physical, or emotional need, I want to be there; someone you can depend upon." Alonzo paused to allow Pauline to respond.

"I think that is important. I can support that," Pauline nodded her head in agreement. "I don't think you'll want to hear about my family problems. That would be hard to discuss without it becoming," Pauline paused, "what did you call it? Gospel gushing?"

"Gospel gossip," Alonzo responded.

"Right, gospel gossip. I'll just tell you, it continues to be a mess!" Pauline concluded.

"I know there is tension at home. I do not want you to feel it is necessary to talk about it. Just know, I'm here for you," Alonzo said as he opened his arms with an invitation for a hug.

Pauline felt unusually at peace.

CHAPTER EIGHTEEN
BACON AND CHEESEBURGER?

"So, what was the upshot of the discipleship program? Did Alonzo get the information he was fishing for?" I asked while tapping my pen on the notepad I had been scribbling on.

He chuckled. "I don't think Alonzo was just fishing. I think he had honest intentions; to encourage spiritual growth within the group."

"And get information," I added.

"And, I suppose, to get information." He chuckled again.

"Okay. Well, thus far you've given me very little reason to change my original feelings toward Ol' Sweet & Sour," I concluded. "You've got a young gal involved with a church. Evidently, she was a popular young gal." I'd heard Pauline wasn't hard to look at when she was younger. It was her sour disposition that had altered her appearance. "Who, unfortunately, had a lousy home life. But look, at least she had a group of friends and a youth leader to escape to." I set the pen down as my interest was beginning to wane.

Antonio returned to the table. "Have you two gentlemen made a decision?"

I jokingly responded, "Yes, we're going to stay until we get some food."

Antonio laughed. "And what might it be you'll be having, sir?"

"Just get me a cheeseburger, medium, and can you throw a couple of pieces of bacon on it?"

"So, you want a bacon cheeseburger?" Antonio pointed to the burger under the " Cheeseburger " heading on the menu.

"No," I laughed. "The bacon cheeseburger is more expensive. I just want a cheeseburger with a couple of pieces of bacon on it!"

"I'll see what I can do for you, Mr. Dustin," Antonio responded. "And for you?"

"I'll have the same, uh, medium rare."

"All right, gentlemen. Two cheeseburgers with bacon. Coming right up!" Antonio returned to the kitchen with our orders.

"I'm sorry to be giving you so many details. I simply want you to know more about Pauline," he explained.

"I realize you do. You've said that several times now. But for what reason? What will it change? Anything? You obviously observed Pauline while she was on her best behavior. We were in the den with the beast!" I sighed, attempting to sound less jaded. "At the risk of further repeating myself, what on earth could you possibly share with me that would in any way alter my absolute disgust for her and her son? I watched my wife suffer because of them. I fight the temptation to hate them because of it. We lived it, every day."

"There is nothing I can share to erase your feelings or the fact that she brought suffering to you and your wife." He let out a breath of air as if he'd been holding it for hours.

Conversations at the surrounding tables seemed to flow with ease while we sat, uncomfortably staring at one another, awaiting Antonio's reappearance with our burgers.

"I do hope you'll forgive me. I made a mistake with your order and ordered the bacon and cheeseburger instead of the cheeseburger with bacon. I've modified the price so that it reflects the cheeseburger alone," Antonio said with a smile.

"Well, we'll let it go this time—but I expect more from St. Elmo than this," I said jokingly. "Thank you very much, Antonio."

"My pleasure, Mr. Dustin. Can I get you anything else to drink? More water perhaps?"

"More water would be great. Thanks." I turned my attention back to our conversation as Antonio left our table.

"Okay, okay. If there's more, lay it on me. I've got my bacon cheeseburger now, so I'm happy."

CHAPTER NINETEEN
CAUGHT OFF GUARD
SUNDAY, JUNE 7, 1959

Passing by his open door, Pauline sensed tension. Alonzo's eyes darted from side to side. His brow twitched uncontrollably as if attempting in vain to sort his thoughts. He was otherwise eerily transfixed.

"Alonzo?" she asked. Her soft voice must have penetrated his consciousness like the roar of a cannon in an empty room.

Alonzo exploded from his seat and gasped, "Oh, my gosh! You scared the life out of me!"

"I'm sorry. I didn't mean to startle you. Is... is something wrong?" Pauline held her hands out like she was approaching a nervous dog.

"Wrong? Wrong? Ha, no—no nothing. Nothing at all. Come on in." His visage immediately transformed. It was an awkward transformation. Whatever he was dealing with before Pauline's interruption was masked as he struggled to regain his composure.

Pauline let her arms down and stood in the doorway of his office. Alonzo's transformation was disarming. A sick feeling swept over her. They'd *counseled* together weekly. They'd become good friends. What was this all about? Old suspicions suddenly surfaced. *Was he as fake as her mother? Is everyone fake?*

"Pauline? Come in. Everything is fine." Alonzo struggled to explain. "I just have a few things on my mind and was lost in thought when you arrived. Come on in."

Although her heart told her to believe Alonzo, instinct warned her to keep a distance. It was a feeling she had not felt for a long time —an unintended ability she'd developed to survive her mother's manic behaviors.

"That's okay, Alonzo. I'm just going down the street to Bray's. I'll see you at six." Pauline turned and continued down the hall toward the street. *Something is troubling him. I just know there is.*

At five forty-five, fifty-three high schoolers and their guests piled into the youth room.

Alonzo applauded as one by one the young people continued to pack the room.

"I think we've broken another record this evening! This place is antsville! We're going to have to call Mr. Bray and warn him we will be taking over his fountain on Sunday evenings!"

Everyone applauded.

"Mike, Trina, come on up here, and let's get some music started."

Although Mike and Trina led the singing, Alonzo always selected the songs.

As Alonzo turned to take a seat, his eyes unintentionally locked onto Pauline's. He realized his every move was being scrutinized. He vainly attempted to retain his usual smooth, controlled demeanor, but every attempt felt contrived and mechanical. No one seemed to notice, no one except Pauline.

Nothing appeared out of sorts. The flow of the meeting was just as it was every Sunday evening. Mike played choruses and everyone sang along. An empty plate was passed around the room and was returned just as empty as it had begun. Trina began the piano intro-duction of the last song, "I Know Who Holds Tomorrow."

As the group sang the last phrase of the song, Alonzo stood and began to walk toward the podium. His father and Mr. Hutto repeated this same segue Sunday after Sunday. Alonzo had been tutored well.

"... Many things about tomorrow I don't seem to understand. But I know who holds tomorrow and I know, He holds my hand."

It might not have registered with the others; it did with Pauline. *What an odd song to introduce Alonzo's message.* There was an eerie uncertainty in the words—not an uplifting and encouraging song like Alonzo usually began with. Something did not seem right.

"Hey, gang. First of all, I want you to know how much I love you all." Alonzo paused and jokingly added, "Yes, even you, Danny."

Everyone laughed as Danny stood and took a bow.

"Life is full of uncertainties, isn't it? We try to prepare for them as best we can. Try as we might, we cannot prepare for everything. That is why we must have faith. We must stay close to God, through our devotionals and prayer, through discipleship. Our God is not a God of fear, but a God of faith. Our God is not a God of uncertainty, but a God with a specific plan for each of our lives. He does not want us wandering in the wilderness, but walking faithfully in His way, knowing *'the steps of a good man are ordered by the Lord.'"* Alonzo paused for a moment to lighten the heaviness of his words. *"The steps of a good man are ordered by the Lord."* Come on, gang. Where is that verse found?"

Danny stood and proudly announced, "In the Bible!"

Everyone laughed.

"Thank you, Professor Miller," Alonzo replied.

Pauline quietly raised her hand.

"Yes, Pauline?" Alonzo hesitantly asked.

"Psalm 37:23," Pauline answered.

"Excuse me?" Alonzo was noticeably surprised by Pauline's response.

"The verse you quoted is from Psalm 37," Pauline replied. "The steps of a good man—or woman," she added, "are ordered by the Lord and He delighteth in His ways."

"And what do we learn from that verse, Pauline?"

Pauline thought for a moment. "God delights in His perfect plans being faithfully fulfilled, through His children, for His purposes."

The room was silent. It was as if Alonzo and Pauline were in a private discussion, the others—bystanders—unintentionally eavesdropped.

"Yes, yes, Pauline. His plans faithfully fulfilled through His children."

Danny broke the silence, "Well, it's in the Bible, isn't it?"

"Yes, Danny. Yes, I'll have to admit, you were correct! It IS in the Bible," Alonzo replied through a light chuckle.

Pauline glanced toward Marc. Their eyes immediately met as he gave her a wink and a nod. His lips formed the words, *"Nice job!"*

She returned her focus to the front, making no further overture of acknowledgment toward Marc.

"Gang, God's plans are not always what we expect. Think of it this way. The prophet Isaiah lived 700 years before the birth of Jesus and yet, in Isaiah chapter 53, he wrote in detail about the crucifixion. The Jews were looking for a victorious warrior—that wasn't God's plan. Jesus came as a suffering servant."

Alonzo seemed far more intense and pensive than the youth group had ever witnessed. They hung on his every word.

"Gang, it has always been my intention to remain with you at First Reliance. I love our church—I love you."

Tears formed in Trina's eyes. She stared at the picture of Jesus on the wall, just past where Alonzo stood at the podium. She fought the urge to blink knowing to do so would reveal her breaking heart.

Pauline intuitively knew what had been troubling him—Alonzo was announcing he was leaving.

"Yesterday morning, I received a letter of acceptance from Augustana College. It's my dad's alma mater. I'd forgotten all about submitting my application. Frankly, I was shocked when it came in the mail. God's plans are not always what we expect."

No one said a word, but Alonzo could sense emotions were intensifying.

"I know, I, I know you must have questions. Heck, I have questions. I want to be open with you, so please feel free to ask."

No one responded. No one moved. There was a universal sense of betrayal. Alonzo was their leader, their friend, and their youth pastor.

"Guys, gals, this isn't the end of the world. This is the beginning of something bigger, better!"

Pauline showed no emotion. Her eyes did not move from his and as much as he tried, his eyes could not escape hers. He continued his attempts to explain to the group his need to leave. It made little difference. They felt betrayed and used. They wondered if he'd ever really cared or if his position was simply a springboard in his career as a minister.

Alonzo sensed their feelings of mistrust. He nervously tapped the lectern.

"To be involved in ministry I have to continue my education. This is an opportunity to better prepare me for eventually having my own church. Honestly, I did not anticipate this letter, and I know you are disappointed. Mine is a mixture of disappointment and anticipation. It wasn't my plan, but evidently, it is God's."

Alonzo was prepared to make this difficult announcement. His shaky breaths indicated he had not prepared for the youth group's response. "Okay, look. This isn't happening tomorrow. I mean, I don't start until next year!"

Every young person in attendance joined in Pauline's glare. Everyone stared directly through Alonzo, piercing his heart. He lifted his chin to pull the tears back from his eyes and stuttered through his words. "Why don't we stand together, form a circle, and pray as God leads?"

No one moved.

"Okay then. How about we sing? Let's lift our hearts in song; how about that?"

One by one every member of Alonzo's youth group, and every guest stood, but they would not be singing. Danny was the first to walk out the door. Jerry followed as did everyone in the group. Marc and Pauline were the only ones left in the room.

"Marc, I'm really sorry. This isn't the way—"

"Naw, it's okay, Alonzo," Marc replied. "Sometimes God's plans are not what we expect, right? It's cool." Marc left the room.

Pauline and Alonzo were alone. She moved toward the door, and Alonzo begged, "Pauline, I hope you can understand the situation I am in. My Dad—"

She interrupted. "Stop! I don't. I can't. Don't say anymore! You've already left us."

CHAPTER TWENTY
AFTER THE EVENING SERVICE
JUNE 7, 1959

Their sense of rejection was palpable. The First Reliance Baptist Youth Group quietly huddled together in the back of the church. There would be no ice-cream social tonight.

Mr. Kurdzuk approached the huddle. "You're going to have to move along. We're turning off all the lights."

No one moved.

"Hey. Did you hear me? Service is over. It's time for you kids to go home."

Pastor Al approached the cortege. "Hey, kids. Why all the long faces?" He turned to Mr. Kurdzuk, "Howard, it's okay. I've got this. Check all the lights for me. I'll make sure the doors are all locked before I leave."

Trina sobbed into Danny's shoulder. Danny loosened his grip, but Trina held tighter. Danny responded with a reassuring squeeze. His eyes met the eyes of Pastor Al. No words were exchanged; no words needed to be exchanged.

"Kids, I don't know what is going on. Do you want to talk about something? You always have me; you always have Alonzo—"

"Liar!" Trina cried.

"Whoa; wait a minute! What is this all about? That is totally inappropriate, young lady."

Danny interrupted, "No you wait a minute, Pastor Al—you wait! Is Alonzo moving away? Is he going to school? Yes, or no?"

The question caught Pastor Al off balance. "Well, he has to continue his education to properly prepare himself for his calling."

Danny continued, "Right! So, did you lie? Didn't you say we would have him when we all know we won't? And who are we? Aren't *we* his calling? Aren't we at least a part of it? What happens to us?" Danny sniffed. "We know what's gonna happen." He jutted his chin in the direction where Mr. Kurdzuk had been standing. "A bunch of old men are going to get together in a private meeting and decide who will be best for us. We won't have any say in the decision, will we? We're just kids—right?"

Danny was not backing down. "We don't want a babysitter. We don't want someone they select. We don't want to be watched, protected, or controlled. Right now, we just want what you gave us —we want to be alone! Come on, gang. Let's get outta here."

Danny and Trina turned and walked to the parking lot. Everyone followed, leaving Pastor Al standing alone.

Pastor Al was deeply troubled by the confrontation. He hurriedly checked all the doors and made his way to the parsonage.

"Is everything all right?" Anna asked.

"I had a little run-in with the youth group. Lon? Lon, get in here."

"What do you mean a run-in?" she asked.

"I'll tell you about it." He turned his attention back to Alonzo. "Lonnie, I'm calling you."

Alonzo appeared in the hallway. "I'm sorry, Dad. I was finishing up a telephone call. What's up?"

"That's what I'd like to know. What's up with the youth group?"

Again, Pastor Al's wife joined the conversation. "What is wrong with the youth group, dear?"

"They were all congregating outside the church. I could tell something was wrong. When I approached them, one of the boys all but attacked me. What did you tell them?"

Alonzo's heart sank. "Dad, it was terrible. I was teaching about God's will and how everything happens for a purpose. I told them I would be going back to school to continue my education—it didn't go over well."

"I'll say it didn't! They called me a liar then turned and walked away. Absolutely no respect whatsoever!"

"Dad, what did you say to them?"

"I told you. I saw that there was a problem and wanted to help. I told them they could always count on you and me."

"Well, with all due respect, Dad, that wasn't true. Sure, I'm here for them right now, but they know I will be leaving. Who will they have then?"

"Yeah, that's what they asked." Pastor Al sat down on the sofa and motioned for Alonzo to sit across from him.

"Dad, these are great young people. They are hurt, that's all. They didn't mean to disrespect you. They walked out on me too."

"Lon, what are we going to do? This type of thing cannot be allowed to fester. It's just the opportunity Satan looks for to step in and upset the entire applecart!"

Alonzo had to chuckle at the metaphor. "Satan's still into apples, huh Dad?"

"Son, this is nothing to take lightly. I want you to call every child in that group and talk with them—individually. I want their parents' names, and I'll contact their parents."

"Okay. I'll call every one of them." Alonzo stood up. "Dad? These are not children. You and every other adult at First Reliance have to change the way you think about the youth—the way you refer to them. These are young adults faced with worldly influences you could not even imagine."

"I know this," Pastor Al began. "The deacons are going to have to put together a search committee to find a replacement for you as soon as possible."

"Dad, aren't you reacting to the situation rather than responding to it? There's plenty of time to find a replacement before I leave for school. If it gets out you've already begun the search, you'll lose the youth group's trust for sure."

"I'm not worried about losing their trust—they're kids! I'm concerned about the fallout we could have with their parents. There's a business side to the ministry, son. These people are supporting the church, the running of the church, and the extended ministries of the church. I don't want this to get out of hand."

"Dad, I told you, I understand. I will be on this first thing tomorrow."

"Lon, I want you to write a script. Let's go over it together before you contact the kids."

"The youth group, Dad. It's the youth group."

Alonzo returned to his bedroom and typed out a brief script.

The next morning Alonzo found his mom and dad where they were every Monday morning, in the garage, bundling newspapers and separating bottles to be reclaimed for cash. "Good morning, Mom. Hey, Dad. I put together a little script for you to look at."

"Good morning, sweetheart," His mother replied.

"Set it on the table in the kitchen. I'll take a look at it as soon as we've finished bundling and stacking these papers," Pastor Al said.

"Dad, if you don't mind, I'd like you to take a look at it right now. If I have to make changes, I don't want to be making them at the last minute. This telephone call needs to flow naturally."

Alonzo's dad began to tie the stack of papers he was working on. "Come over here. Let me borrow your finger so I can cinch this thing up, and I'll take a look."

Alonzo obliged, then handed his dad the brief script.

Hi gang, this is Alonzo. Is this a good time to call?

I want to talk with you about my schooling next year and answer any questions you have. I assure you, when that time comes, the youth group will have a say in who is selected to be my replacement.

I know this change isn't easy. It isn't easy for me either. I'm counting on you, your leadership, to help me during the transition.

So, what concerns you?

"Lon, you can't tell the kids they will select your replacement. That's the responsibility of the selection committee."

"Dad, I didn't say they would select my replacement. I said they would have a say in who is selected."

"Well, you'll have to change that. These are kids, Lonnie. They don't know the first thing about the business of the church."

"Dad, you can't continue to refer to them as kids. They are young people; they are not kids, not in the way you think of them or say it. If we are going to grow a youth group that makes an impact upon the community, if we are going to raise leaders, we are going to have to give these young people some respect and some responsibility."

"And THAT, my son, is why you are continuing your education. The notion that these, these, young people, as you call them, are mature enough to participate in church business is absurd."

"And at what age are they ready? When, Dad? Does it just happen or is there a special age?"

His mother interrupted. "Lonnie, watch the tone of your voice. You are talking to your father."

"Am I, Mom? Am I? Or am I talking to my pastor? I'm sorry if my tone is offensive, but maybe the tone of my voice needs to change a little. Maybe then I will be heard—or am I still a kid?"

"Alonzo!" his mom gasped.

"Alonzo, I want you to change that part of your script. The rest is fine the way it is."

"Why do I even try to please you—Pastor?"

Alonzo's father appeared unscathed by Alonzo's comment. "You shouldn't." He said nonchalantly. "You should desire to please God."

Another zinger. Alonzo shook his head and returned to his bedroom.

CHAPTER TWENTY-ONE
THE TELEPHONE CALL
JUNE 1959

"Hi, Danny. This is Alonzo. Is this a good time to call?"

"Hi, Alonzo. I guess, I guess I'm in trouble, huh? I'm sorry about last night. It's just..."

Alonzo continued. "No, no. You are not in trouble. I want to talk with you about my schooling next year and answer any questions you have."

"Questions? We all have questions, Alonzo. Why didn't you tell us you were applying? It's just not going to be the same without you." Danny sighed. "You never said you were applying. It's like, like you were keeping a secret from us. How do we know your dad doesn't have his own secrets? How do we know he hasn't already selected someone?"

"Danny, I am sorry I didn't tell the group about my application. It wasn't a secret. I never thought my application would even be considered, let alone accepted. There was no reason to worry everyone."

"Yeah, I get it."

Although Danny was the class clown, Alonzo could tell he was trying to be understanding. "I assure you; no one has been selected to take my place. To my knowledge, no one other than our youth group knows about my leaving."

Danny scoffed. "Well, you're wrong on that one, Alonzo. We talked all night about it. We all met over at Paige's house. Her mom called everyone's parents to tell them we were there and why. By this time, everyone in the church knows about it."

"I know this change isn't easy. It isn't easy for me either. I'm counting on you, your leadership, to help me during the transition. I'm calling everyone to talk to each one personally."

"I wouldn't do that, Alonzo," Danny said.

"Why not?"

"We're your GROUP. Talk to us as a group. We'll be honest with you. Besides, what I am telling you is the same thing everyone else will say. If we all hear it at the same time, we all hear it from you; no misunderstandings, no rumors."

Alonzo thought to himself, *and Dad considers them just kids.* "You're right, Danny. Look, there's no school, so let's take this coming Wednesday afternoon and discuss it as a group—no matter how long it takes. Will you let the gang know about the Wednesday meeting?"

"Sure, I will. What time?"

"Let's say two o'clock?"

"Okay, two o'clock. Alonzo? I'm sorry for disrespecting your dad. Trina is sorry for calling him a liar. Is your dad going to be at our meeting Wednesday afternoon?"

"No, Danny. No, he will not be invited. We have things to work out together. This is between the youth group and me. If he mentions coming, I will ask him not to come."

"And he'll listen?"

Alonzo remained quiet.

"Will he listen to you, Alonzo?"

"Danny, you have my word. I will see to it that he does not show up at our meeting."

CHAPTER TWENTY-TWO
POTATO SALAD
JUNE 1959

"Mom, your potato salad is ready," Pauline announced.

"It better be good! I hope you didn't put too many onions in it this time," Elizabeth screeched.

"You're welcome, Mom," Pauline sarcastically sang, shaking her head in disbelief.

At eleven o'clock the telephone rang.

"I'll get it, Mom." Pauline lifted the handset from the telephone on the wall. "Hello?"

"Hi, Pauline?"

"Marc?" Pauline's voice rose a couple of octaves.

"Yeah. Is it, is it okay for me to call?"

"Hi, Marc! Oh, my goodness. Hello. Yes! Yes, it's fine for you to call. How are you?"

"I didn't know if... if it was okay. I mean, with you and Jerry and all."

"Marc, Jerry Pennypacker is just a friend. There is nothing serious between us at all," Pauline laughingly replied.

"Well, to be honest, I think *there would be* if Jerry had his way," Marc concluded.

Pauline laughed again. "Ain't that a bite! I don't know if what you are saying is true, but if it is, Jerold Pennypacker is going to be very disappointed," Pauline stifled the chuckle and took a more serious tone. "Regardless of what *anyone* says, Jerry is just a friend."

The doorbell disrupted Pauline.

Elizabeth walked into the kitchen putting on her hat and adjusting her gloves. She then went to the refrigerator and removed the potato salad. "I'm on my way to ladies' luncheon." She exited the kitchen and made her way to the front door, then she quickly turned to Pauline. "Clean up this house before your father gets home and make sure you dust and put out clean doilies. Pauline? Pauline, did you hear me?"

"Bye, Mom. Love you oodles," Pauline replied with a dismissive roll of her eyes.

From the front porch, Pauline could hear her mother shout, "And don't be on that telephone all day!"

"I'm sorry, Marc. That was my mom. She's—well, she's a mom. What were you saying?"

"I'm sorry, there was no ice-cream social Sunday night. I was looking forward to it."

"I was too. I don't know if there will ever be another ice-cream social or if anything will ever be the same," Pauline replied. "I missed visiting with you." Pauline paused just long enough to give the impression she'd divulged more than she intended. "I mean, I'm sure everyone missed visiting with you."

"Thanks; I missed being there. Ya know, every time I think I'm going to get a chance to say hello to you something..." Marc swallowed, "or *someone* interrupts."

Pauline now cradled the receiver with both hands listening intently to Marc's every word, *someone*. Perhaps Marc was referring to Paige. Pauline was interested in Marc, but not enough to create an issue with her best friend. "Well, what should we do about that?" Pauline asked. A feeling of invincibility buzzed from the phone into her hands and slowly pulsed through her bloodstream.

Marc jumped at the opportunity. "How about we go over to Bray's this afternoon, for a soda or something? It'll make up for missing the ice-cream social."

He certainly knows how to call the plays, Pauline thought. "Well, I got a call from Danny. Alonzo is having a special meeting with the youth group this afternoon," Pauline responded.

"Well, I'm not a member. Is it something you need to attend?" Marc asked.

Pauline thought about it. The meeting wouldn't change the fact that Alonzo was leaving. *It will probably be another manipulation to make everyone feel guilty for being upset,* she thought. "Tell ya what. How 'bout I meet you there?" she asked.

"I can pick you up!" Marc insisted.

"No, I think it will be better if we go separately. I don't want to start any rumors."

"Okay by me. I'll meet you at Bray's around three o'clock?"

"Three o'clock." Pauline glanced up at the kitchen wall clock. "Three o'clock will be perfect! I'll see you then," Pauline responded.

Pauline gently tossed the handset into its cradle and hurried up the stairs. The handset clipped the front of the cradle and plunged toward the floor. It bounced against the linoleum and sprang back toward the cradle. The cord recoiled, but the handset missed the cradle by fourteen inches. It repeated its unassisted attempts several more times before dangling and spinning three inches above the green linoleum kitchen floor.

Attendance at the ladies' luncheon was overwhelming. Elizabeth immediately realized it would be hours before the luncheon concluded. She excused herself and went into the church office to call home. Pauline would have to begin dinner preparations.

Elizabeth reached for the phone. She called the house to order Pauline to work on dinner.

Pauline continued to primp until her hair and makeup were complete. She chose to wear her favorite pleated red skirt and draped her torso with a white Angora sweater, tastefully accentuating her figure.

"*Get off the telefono!*" Elizabeth yelled into the handset. Her repeated attempts to call the house were unsuccessful. Her threatening tone was challenged by the obstinate and equally determined tone of the busy signal.

A saucy smile emerged from Pauline's lips as she examined her image in the mirror. With her hands on her hips, she turned from side to side flinging her skirt in suggestive innocence. "Okay, Mr. Joshua-Marc Romano. It's time to melt some ice cream."

Pauline hurried out the kitchen door never noticing the pendulous handset.

In the church's office, Elizabeth replaced the handset and returned to her place at the luncheon table.

"Is everything all right, Liz?" Margaret Clamson asked.

"Oh, I'm sure everything is fine, Madge. Our telephone line has been busy, and I can't get through to Pauline. I just worry about her sometimes. No matter how old your kids get, a mother worries. The teenage years can be difficult. I do my best to keep our relationship open, but Pauline can be difficult at times," Elizabeth replied in feigned concern.

"Liz, you are a wonderful mother. Why, I just look at all the things you do for your girls. And you still devote yourself to so many worthwhile causes. Elizabeth Bianchi, Reliance would do well to have more women like you, dear."

"Madge, that's so very nice of you to say. Yes, we do our best to serve others." Elizabeth smiled as she reached for the potato salad.

"Care for some potato salad? It took me the better part of the morning to prepare it." Placing her hand on Margaret's wrist, Elizabeth whispered, "I hope everyone enjoys it."

Her mock humility was met with precisely the comment she encouraged.

"Liz, my dear, how do you do it? It is absolutely glorious." Margaret declared in amazement.

CHAPTER TWENTY-THREE
RENDEZVOUS AT BRAY'S
JUNE 1959

"Hi, Mr. Bray," Pauline announced as she entered Bray's Pharmacy.

"Well, hello, pretty lady," Mr. Bray responded. "Aren't you a fine sight to see!"

"Thank you, sir."

"Is there something I can help you with today?" he asked.

"No, I'm waiting for someone. We're going to get a soda, I think."

"That someone wouldn't be Jerry Pennypacker, would it?" Mr. Bray teased as he looked over his glasses and smiled.

"No, it wouldn't! Why does everyone think I'm keen on Jerry Pennypacker?" Pauline bristled.

Mr. Bray chuckled. "Maybe because you get so defensive when his name is mentioned."

The clanging of the brass doorbell hanging on the front door signaled the entrance of another customer.

Pauline swiftly turned in hopeful anticipation. Her smile was gratefully received by eighty-three-year-old Myrtle Fierstein. "Well, hello, my dear. What a beautiful smile. How are you today?"

Pauline's plummeting countenance wasn't masked by her

cheerful response. "Oh, hello, Miss Fierstein. I'm, I'm doing very well, uh, thank you. How are you?" As soon as Pauline's words escaped her lips, she realized her blunder and vainly tried to reel in her question.

Everyone in Marion County knew better than to ask Miss Fierstein how she was. You could tell her she looked well, tell her she looked young and vibrant. You could compliment her hair, her dress, her hat, or her shoes, but NEVER, EVER, ask her how she was! Miss Fierstein would tell you. Miss Fierstein would tell you everything.

"Oh, I'm just not doing very well, I'm afraid. You know, ever since Jesse passed, I haven't been well. My doctors tell me they can't find anything wrong with me, but I know I don't have long on this old earth; it could be any time now. I just struggle through each day. You know my back was never the same after carrying Jesse to the car. The old dog had no more life in him. Now I know how he must have felt. Getting old is no fun, my dear, no fun at all. Everything just falls apart. My eyesight is failing. You are so young and pretty. You wouldn't understand how hard it is for me to read. I can't even see my prescriptions."

Mr. Bray pulled the feather duster from his belt and frantically dusted the first row of apples as he hastily retreated from the register and Miss Fierstein's conversation with Pauline.

"No, my dear. Life holds no more pleasures for an old woman. Have I told you about my back? It was never the same after Jesse passed—"

"Yes, yes Miss Fierstein," Pauline interrupted. "You've told me how you hurt your back carrying Jesse to the car. I am very sorry for your loss. That was quite a few years ago, wasn't it?"

Another mistake! NEVER prolong the conversation by asking Miss Fierstein a question.

"Well, yes, my dear. It will be four years in three months. But you wouldn't understand the loss. It seems like yesterday when I came home and found him lying helpless on the kitchen floor. That's what will happen to me—you just watch. Someone will find me alone at home, lifeless. Then they'll understand. They won't tell me I'm well then. You know, those doctors don't know everything. They haven't lived as long as I've lived. Arthritis keeps me in constant pain. Did I tell you about my..."

Pauline was trapped. Miss Fierstein had an unusual ability to seemingly continue talking without taking a breath. When she did take a breath, she ended every sentence with the words, *but, so, and.*

Realizing the predicament he'd left Pauline in, conviction gripped Mr. Bray and he reluctantly made his way back to the front counter.

"Myrtle, my dear! You look as lovely as a fresh bouquet of daisies! It's good to see you doing so well!"

Miss Fierstein bristled. "Well, I'm not *doing so well*! I'm not well at all!"

"Well, you certainly wouldn't know it by your glorious countenance!" Mr. Bray retorted.

With that, Miss Fierstein abruptly turned and left the store without making a purchase.

"Oh, my gosh, Mr. Bray. You saved my life! Thank you," Pauline whispered with relief. "I'm sorry she didn't buy anything."

"Oh, don't worry, my dear. She'll be back." He shook his head in disgust. "She always comes back."

Mr. Bray leaned forward. After a glance to his left and right, in a hushed tone, he asked, "Did I ever tell you about the pain in my right hip?"

Pauline panicked. *Oh, no, not you, too!* she thought.

Mr. Bray laughed. His eyes darted over Pauline's shoulder and out the window. "This fella you are meeting wouldn't be driving a light blue Chevy, would he?"

"That's him. That's him, Mr. Bray. How do I look?" Pauline asked as she ran her fingers over the pleats in her skirt.

"You look strikingly beautiful. In fact, if you were my daughter, I wouldn't let you out of the house!"

"Oh, you're just being silly. But I look okay, don't I?"

"Pauline, you look beautiful." Mr. Bray leaned forward as the front door opened and whispered, "He's not a bad-looking fella either. I'll go back to the fountain and set up a couple of places for you at the soda bar, okay?"

"That will be peachy, Mr. Bray. Thank you," Pauline replied.

"Hi, Pauline!" Marc confidently strode into the shop.

"Hi, Marc. Fancy meeting you here!" They both laughed.

"Thanks for meeting me on such short notice."

"It was no problem at all. I'm glad we finally have a chance to visit," Pauline replied.

"Why don't we get a soda or some ice cream at the fountain?" Marc asked.

"That would be great."

Mr. Bray directed the couple to a prepared setting at the bar. "Here you go, you two. I've got you all set up at the soda bar."

"Marc, this is Mr. Bray. Mr. Bray, this is Marc." Having forgotten Marc's last name, she hung on to his first name and looked back at him for a little help.

"Romano, Marc Romano. It's a pleasure to meet you, Mr. Bray."

"Well, it's nice to meet you, son. Are you new to the area or just visiting?"

"We're new. My family just moved here from Burlington County a couple of months ago."

"And this is your first time at Bray's Market?" Mr. Bray asked, as if deeply hurt.

"Well, there has to be a first time. But I assure you, it won't be the last," Marc responded.

"You two take a look at the menu. I'll get you a couple of waters. We've got every flavor of ice cream on the menu. If you'd like, I'll heat you some of Mrs. Bray's hot fudge. Marc, her fudge alone will make you want to come back. Take your time, kids." Mr. Bray chuckled as he went back to some dusting.

"Thank you, sir," Marc replied.

CHAPTER TWENTY-FOUR
THE MEETING
JUNE 1959

It was two o'clock, and the room was packed. There were young people present whom Alonzo had not seen in months. As they entered the room, they signed a roster. It was best to have an accurate record of everyone in attendance. Those who were unable to attend would be receiving a personal visit from Alonzo.

"Good afternoon, everyone. I guess we all know why we're here. Let's start with prayer and then I want to open the meeting to any and all of your questions and comments." The room fell silent. "Lord, the afternoon is yours; these people are yours; our future is yours. Guide us in a way that honors you. Amen." After the amens, Alonzo cleared his throat. "Guys, gals, I have nothing to say in advance of your questions. We all know I am going back to school, and my leaving will have an impact on every one of us. This is your time. The floor is yours."

The questions were as Alonzo expected. They were good questions; there were probing questions. Alonzo responded to each question directly, openly, and honestly. He made certain not to appear preachy or in any way manipulative.

Jerry spoke up, "So, are we going to have a say in who replaces you?"

"Jerry, that's the burning question right now. I believe you should have a say. I've been giving it some thought. How does this sound? Let's work together to establish our own guidelines. I can work on the structure, but the guidelines will totally be yours."

For the first time, there seemed to be cohesion. Alonzo would set up a variety of meetings, allowing every aspect of Christian service to be addressed. It would be a learning experience, a growth experience for everyone in the group.

"When you have completed your guidelines, we will, as a group, submit them to whoever is interviewing candidates. The candidates will receive a copy of your guidelines to be prepared for their interviews, and, more importantly, they will know what you are looking for in a youth director."

Trina interjected, "How will we know they got the suggestions? What makes you so sure the deacons, or whoever won't just set them aside and forget about us?"

"Trina, it's a fair question. Before the candidate is hired, they will have to meet with the entire youth group. During that meeting, you will be able to determine how much of your voice was heard during the interview process and how much of an impact you had on the candidate's selection."

The youth group all nodded in agreement.

"Are there any more questions or comments?" Alonzo asked.

Jerry stood up. "Alonzo. Thank you for this afternoon. Thank you for listening to us and treating us like adults. We can work this out together. Besides, if the deacons don't listen to us, we might write a few guidelines for them too!"

Everyone laughed.

"Hey, I contacted Mr. Bray. He and Mrs. Bray will open the fountain for us if we promise to control Danny!"

There was light laughter. Paige glanced at Danny who was tilting his head and framing an innocent grin between his thumbs and fore-fingers.

Seeing the expression on Danny's face, Paige asked, "Hey Alonzo? Did you set up a second option besides Bray's—just in case?"

The laughter continued.

"Come on gang! Let's get some ice cream!" Alonzo said.

Pauline and Marc were just finishing their double malt when Alonzo arrived.

Pauline panicked. "Oh, no! Marc, what are we going to do?"

"Pauline, keep calm. I'll take care of this." Marc quickly pulled his straw from their shared malt and shoved it in the glass of water in front of him. The convicting haze of malt mingling with his water was a dead giveaway. He picked up the glass and downed its murky contents before the youth group made their way to the fountain.

"We're going to have to meet on the sly from now on!" Marc whispered.

"Hey! What are you two doing here?" Alonzo asked, eyeing Pauline.

"Hi, Alonzo," Marc said in a cool and calm tone. "Just having a malt."

Alonzo didn't take his eyes off Pauline, "We just finished our youth group meeting."

Pauline bit her lip and looked down at her pleats to make sure they were straight. "I forgot. Was that today?"

Marc asked, "How was it?"

"It was great, Marc. The meeting was very good. I'm sorry you guys missed it. Maybe we can get together later, and I'll fill you in." Alonzo shoved his hands in his pockets just as the youth group began filing in the door. Each youth acknowledged Mr. Bray, who returned the greetings to each person by name.

"Sure, Alonzo. Let's do that. Hey gang," Marc said.

"Hey, Marc. Hi, Pauline," the group echoed.

The group crowded around the fountain. Their banter drew attention away from Pauline and Marc. Their rendezvous, however, did not go unnoticed by Paige.

Paige moved in behind Pauline. Like an angry ventriloquist, Paige's lips did not move as she whispered, "What are you doing here?"

Without hesitation, Pauline innocently replied, "Having a malt. What are you going to get?"

"You know what I mean. What are you doing here with Marc?" Page hissed.

"Marc?" Pauline nervously laughed. "Oh, Paige. Cool your jets! Marc was here, and I just happened to join him. Come on. Sit down and get some ice cream."

Pauline moved away from Marc to where Jerry was seated.

Alonzo quietly watched the exchange. Instinctively, he knew there was more going on. He would wait for his meeting with Pauline to get answers.

CHAPTER TWENTY-FIVE

SO, DID ALONZO FOLLOW UP?

"So, did Alonzo follow up with Pauline? Did he continue having meetings with her?" I asked.

"He did. The next meeting set in motion a sequence of events that changed the lives of everyone involved. Keep in mind, Alonzo was the youth director, but he was only eighteen. He'd only been out of high school a year before assuming his position and the responsibility in his dad's church. In Pastor Ricci's mind, it was a foregone conclusion, Alonzo would one day be the senior pastor in his own church. The number of young people in the youth group at First Reliance was growing. They were without a youth director, so hiring Alonzo provided the necessary leadership for them while allowing Pastor Al the opportunity to supervise and direct his son's early ministry."

"Do you think that was wrong?" I took a swig of water to wash down my latest bite of bacon burger.

"I think it was premature."

"You said the next meeting changed the lives of everyone involved. That's quite a provocative statement."

"I don't say it to be provocative, though it might be. I am suggesting that had Pauline and Marc attended the first meeting, things might have gone in an entirely different direction."

CHAPTER TWENTY-SIX

FOLLOW-UP MEETING
JUNE 1959

"Hello?" Elizabeth answered the phone in a silky tone reserved for those she wished to impress.

"Hi, Mrs. Bianchi. This is Alonzo. Is Pauline available?"

"Hello, Alonzo. I heard a disturbing rumor that you will be leaving us soon. Is this true?"

"Well, yes. Yes, I will be going back to school, continuing my education."

"How soon before you leave? I'm sure the children are devastated."

"The youth group is dealing with this in a very mature manner, Mrs. Bianchi. I'm proud of them. If she is available, can I speak with Pauline?" Alonzo asked in a clipped tone.

"Oh, certainly, dear. Certainly." Elizabeth covered the receiver just enough to muffle her voice but not enough to hide her call to Pauline.

"Pauline? Pauline sweetheart. Alonzo Ricci is on the telephone for you. Sweetheart? Did you hear me?"

"Okay, Mom; I'm coming." Her mother's theatrical saccharine tone sickened her.

Taking the receiver from her mother, Pauline offered an equally spurious smile. "Hello?" Pauline said into the receiver.

"Hi, Pauline. It's Alonzo. How are you doing?"

"I'm fine, I guess. How are you?"

"Ha! I'm always fine. Listen, you missed a great meeting, but I'm glad we hooked up with you and Marc at Bray's. I want to fill you in on what we talked about and what was decided. Could we get together sometime tomorrow to visit?"

Pauline offered a hesitant response. "All right. What time is best for you?"

"How about tomorrow at, let's say, four o'clock?"

"Okay, four o'clock tomorrow. Where do you want to meet?"

"I'll be working at the church. Let's just meet in my office if that's okay with you."

"Four o'clock in your office. Got it. I'll see you then." Pauline hung up the telephone.

"What did he want?" Elizabeth yelled from the living room.

"He just wants to meet with me, Mom." Pauline was in no mood for her mother's saltiness.

"What did you do now?"

"Nothing, Mother! He just wants to talk to me about what the group is planning to do about his leaving."

"What do mean, 'what the group is planning to do?' He's leaving! The group isn't going to do anything about it."

"Okay, Mom. Is that all?"

"You watch what you say, young lady. You just sit there, listen, and then politely leave. Do you understand me?"

"Do I understand you? Of course, I understand you. I speak English fluently."

Pauline pulled into the church parking lot at three forty-five, parked the car, and walked down the long corridor leading to the youth room and Alonzo's office. His office door was open. Alonzo was seated at his desk. Pauline quietly reached around the threshold and knocked on the already-opened door.

"Hi, Pauline! Thank you for coming over. Sit down, sit down. Make yourself comfortable on the old cow!"

Pauline laughed, "Do you think your replacement will keep this old couch?"

"If he does, they are either not paying him enough, or he's not planning on staying very long!" Alonzo replied.

"Pauline, why didn't you come to the meeting Wednesday afternoon?"

Why waste time on chit-chat? Pauline thought. "I didn't come because I'm mad at you. I trusted you, Alonzo, and then out of nowhere, you tell me you are leaving."

"Pauline. My going back to school has nothing to do with my relationship with you or anyone in the youth group." Alonzo was surprised by her frankness. "Can you forgive me?"

"Forgive you? For what? Doing what you say God is telling you to do? How dumb would that be?"

"I'm sorry. I can't think of the right words to say."

"Well, you should. You're my youth director. You always have answers. You're the one who asked me to come over. You wanted to talk to me, remember? You're supposed to always have the right words to say—aren't you?"

Pauline would not be easily dissuaded. Alonzo broached the question—she'd truthfully responded. Any attempt to assuage her position would now be met with a seldom exposed belligerence.

"Pauline, it's different. I am sorry to hurt your feelings. I know things are not good for you at home, and I'm sorry to add to your disappointment."

"My home has nothing to do with this! Why would you even bring my home up? Forget it. There is nothing you can do. There's nothing I expect you to do. That's life, right? *'All things work together for good,' blah, blah, blah,* right?"

"Pauline, they do. Everything happens for a reason. Look, I have my own challenges being the preacher's kid. Sometimes the pressure to perform is beyond what I can take. My dad is a Godly man, but living with him is like living in a pressure cooker every moment of every day. I don't get a dad. Instead, I have a live-in judge, jury, and executioner. Oh, I forgot—and pastor!"

Pauline leaned back and shook her head.

Alonzo shook his head. "No, no. I'm sorry. I shouldn't be complaining like this. I'm sorry. Besides, you have your own problems. I want to continue supporting you for as long as I'm here."

"What? I'm supposed to feel sorry for you? Poor Alonzo has to go to college. Poor Alonzo, his daddy is the preacher. Poor Alonzo, poor Alonzo, poor Alonzo, poor Alonzo." Pauline paused to take a deep breath. "You're an idiot!" The words were uncomfortably familiar to Pauline. She could not believe they escaped her lips. She wiped her mouth with the back of her hand to hide her shock, Pauline continued. "You do what you have to do. Don't worry about me. Take care of your issues. You've got enough. I'll take care of mine—"

Alonzo interrupted, "Maybe I am an idiot, but I do worry about you, Pauline. I'm still here if you need me. I haven't left. Please, don't hesitate to come to me. My office door will always be open for you."

"Right." Pauline stood in the doorway, ready to exit. Alonzo opened his arms for a parting hug. As awkward as it seemed, she wanted that hug. She needed the security, the honesty of a hug from someone who might care. But there was no way she was going to give in and make the situation easier for Alonzo. She stared at Alonzo awkwardly standing with outstretched arms.

"Pauline, I will be here for you."

"Thanks, Alonzo, but let's face it, you will be here—until you're not." She turned to exit. "I gotta go." Pauline abruptly left the office.

That did not go well, he thought. *That did not go well at all.*

Pauline felt a sense of satisfaction. She'd avoided Alonzo's recap of Wednesday's meeting—a meeting she wasn't interested in attending in the first place. She'd also avoided his criticism for not attending.

Pauline walked to Bray's Pharmacy to the telephone booth she and Marc had surreptitiously used to communicate. The telephone rang once, twice, and then stopped ringing. It was their agreed-upon signal. If Marc was home, he would return the call. Pauline retrieved her dime and waited for Marc's call.

"Hello?"

"Hey, I'm glad you called. Is everything okay?" Marc asked.

"I just wanted to warn you. If he hasn't already called, Alonzo will be calling to set up a meeting with you."

"A meeting? About what?"

"To tell you what the youth group decided during their Wednesday afternoon meeting."

Marc laughed. "I thought they decided to get some ice cream."

"No, Marc. I'm serious. I just left Alonzo's office. I told him how angry I am, and I never gave him a chance to preach at me for missing the meeting. I'm not listening to any more well-rehearsed speeches about how I should be supporting him and the group. I've had it with the manipulations."

Marc continued chuckling. It was the first time he'd heard Pauline angry. "Hey, chill out," he chuckled. "I didn't do anything to make you mad. I'm innocent."

"Oh, I'm sorry. It's just... it's just I'm tired of all the hypocrites, the lies, the manipulations!"

"I get it, I get it," Marc responded. "And I'll be careful to be on my best behavior when I'm around you!"

"Stop it, silly. You know what I mean."

"I think I do—but I am one of the newest kids on the block. I'm here with a clean slate. I haven't been around long enough to get riled at anyone." He loudly inhaled. "Well, there was the time Paige walked away with an apple pie she was supposed to deliver. That almost got me riled." He laughed at the memory. His recall was a test to see how Pauline would respond to the mention of Paige.

"If Paige baked it, I am sure it was good. I just called to warn you about Alonzo."

Marc waited for Pauline to continue—but there was silence. "Hello? Hello? Pauline?" Pauline's conversation abruptly ended. "Nice talking to ya," Marc said as he hung up the telephone, chuckling.

Pauline exited the phone booth and growled through clenched jaws, "MEN!"

CHAPTER TWENTY-SEVEN
PAULINE'S REQUEST
JUNE 18, 1959

"Pauline, Pauline? PAULINE!"

She'd heard her mother's call the first time but quietly enjoyed her mother's exasperation at having to call a second and third. "Yes, Mother?"

"Pauline, come down here."

"I'm coming." Pauline bounded down the stairs in reckless abandon, adding to her mother's frustration and all the more fulfilling her amusement. "Did you call me?"

"What do you mean, did I call you? Of course, I called for you. Is there anyone else here named Pauline? Is there anyone else you heard call your name?"

Unfazed, Pauline inquired, "Must have been you then. What is it I can do for you, Mother?"

"You can go over to the church and pick up my bowl from Mrs. Clamson. She said she would leave it on the counter in the fellowship hall. She left me a few other items with it."

"Okie dokie," Pauline said in a flat tone.

"And hurry back! I don't want to find out you were sneaking off with those boys again."

"What boys?"

"Any of them! You just get the bowl and get back here."

The church was just around the corner. Pauline parked the car and made the short walk to the fellowship hall. The door was locked. As much as she didn't want to see Alonzo, Pauline walked down the long corridor toward the youth room. Alonzo's office door was open.

"Excuse me, Alonzo?"

"Hey, Pauline! What brings you over here?"

"My mother wanted me to get her bowl from the fellowship hall. Mrs. Clamson left it there for her, but the door is locked. Do you have a key?" Pauline was all business.

"Sure, I do." Alonzo whispered, "Believe it or not, the pastor trusts me with a master key to the buildings." He laughed at his own response. "Come on, I'll walk you down there."

They walked back toward the fellowship hall. Alonzo did not say another word. The sound of their footsteps echoed in the hall, accentuating the lack of communication.

When they reached the fellowship hall doors, Pauline broke the silence, "So, do you know when the actual date is you will be leaving?"

Alonzo was relieved by her question. "It's too soon to even think about that. I know they'll have an orientation a couple of months before the incoming students begin their first semester."

Pauline softened and asked. "Do you really want to go?"

"Sure, I mean, I know it is what I am supposed to do."

"Yeah, but do you want to go?" Pauline once again asked.

"Pauline, it isn't so much what I want. It's more a matter of what is necessary; it's expected of me."

Pauline looked away, hiding her emotions. "Yeah, I suppose," she muttered.

"Here ya go," Alonzo turned the key and opened the door. "That must be it right over there," he said as he pointed to the long kitchen counter.

"Thanks, Alonzo. Alonzo?" She stopped midstride and turned around.

"Yes?"

"The other day, when we met... I didn't get a chance to tell you I hate to see you go." Pauline paused and smiled. "I was just starting to get to know you."

"Yeah, I was feeling the same way. Why d'ya decide to open up and start meeting with me right before I got my acceptance letter?"

They both laughed.

"I'm sorry for being quiet. I seem to create problems when I open up. It's easier to avoid talking and avoid the problems."

"Well, you haven't created a problem for me, that is, you haven't created a problem for me—yet! We've still got time to get to know one another. That is before you go and goof everything up!" Alonzo teased. Once again, Alonzo laughed.

Pauline joined him in the laughter.

"I'll tell you what. Why don't we grab a soda or something at Bray's some afternoon? We don't always have to meet here at the church," Alonzo suggested.

"That would be wonderful. I'd like that," Pauline responded.

"Just make sure it's not the same day you are going on a hot date with Marc," Alonzo tilted his head sideways. "Or Jerry, or William, or Steve, or Brian, or—"

Pauline slapped his arm. "Stop it, silly! You're beginning to sound like my mother."

"Whoa! I'll be more careful next time!" Once again Alonzo stretched his arms forward inviting a hug. This time Pauline took the opportunity.

"Thanks, Alonzo," she said into his shoulder.

Pauline left the building with her mother's bowl and the assorted items from Mrs. Clamson. Alonzo returned to his office.

Sitting at his desk, reality struck him with a ferocity he did not expect; leaving was going to be painful.

CHAPTER TWENTY-EIGHT
PAIGE AND JERRY
AUGUST 1959

She'd considered her options for weeks. She could go directly to Pauline and ask, or she could go directly to Marc. Either way, she risked losing a friend or losing an opportunity with the man of her dreams. Paige decided to go directly to Jerry Pennypacker.

"Hello?" Jerry answered the call.

"Oh, hi, Jerry. I'm glad you answered the phone. Do you have a couple of minutes to talk?" Paige asked.

"Sure, I do. First of all, who am I talking to?" Jerry responded.

"Oh, my gosh—it's Paige, Paige Cervoni."

"Hiya, Paige. What's cook'n?"

"Look, I don't want to start any rumors or anything, but I wanted to ask you if you noticed Pauline and Marc kind of getting close?"

"Ha! Well, I don't know about them. Pauline and I are certainly not. I can tell you that for a fact!"

"No, really, Jerry. What do you think? Do you think something is going on?"

"Nah, I don't think so. Paige, you've got to stop worrying about Pauline and Marc. Pauline would never do anything to hurt you."

"Is my concern that obvious?"

"Obvious? Ha! Every person in Monroe Township is aware of it! You've got to cool your grilles and just be natural. That's my opinion, anyway."

"Jerry, I like Marc."

"Well, I like Pauline. Maybe you and I should go out together sometime, you know—no strings attached, and see what their response is. I'm not suggesting Marc is bird-dogging me, but, why don't we try?"

There was just enough logic to make the suggestion plausible, but it didn't sit well with her. "I don't want to be a party pooper, but I'm not sure that's the best solution," Paige nervously responded.

"Wait a minute, you called me! Here I am giving you my best idea, and you're being a wet rag."

"I'll think about it, Jerry. Maybe we can sit together at an ice-cream social. I don't know. I'll think about it. So, you don't think anything is going on?"

"I don't know. I mean, I don't think so. Why don't you ask her?"

"I'm not going to ask my best friend if she's trying to steal my guy! What kind of best friend would do that?" Paige was incredulous.

"The same kind of best friend who would be calling another guy and asking if he thought her best friend was stealing her guy!"

"Okay, that's enough from you, Jerold Pennypacker! You're just confusing me," Paige said firmly. Her tone then softened. "Thank you for talking with me. Maybe it's just my imagination."

"A couple of scoops of ice cream might clear things up," Jerry suggested.

"JEROLD!"

CHAPTER TWENTY-NINE

ELIZABETH BIANCHI, OPERATOR

AUGUST 1959

"Hello?" Elizabeth was getting tired of all the attention Pauline was getting.

"Hello, Mrs. Bianchi? This is Marc Romano. Is Pauline available?"

"No, she is not!"

"All right. Will you please—"

Elizabeth slammed the receiver into its carriage.

Five minutes later the telephone rang again. Once again, Elizabeth slammed her magazine onto the coffee table, got up from the couch, and returned to the kitchen to answer it. "Hello?"

"Hello, Mrs. Bianchi? This is Jerry, Jerry Pennypacker. Is Pauline available?"

"No, she is not!"

"Okay, could you—"

Elizabeth once again slammed the receiver into its carriage just as Pauline was coming down the stairs.

"You better be careful, young lady!" Elizabeth's anger momentarily startled Pauline.

"All right, Mother. I'll come down the stairs more slowly," Pauline responded.

"You know what I am talking about—gallivanting around, dragging the Bianchi name through the mud," Elizabeth complained.

"What on earth are you talking about, Mother?"

"You are going to get into trouble, and when you do, don't expect your father and me to protect you!"

"Mother, you are being absurd!"

"Am I? Am I? Boys calling all hours asking for you? You disappear with no word of where you are going or who you are seeing."

"Mother. When have I disappeared without you or Daddy knowing where I was going? And I can't help it if someone calls me. Maybe I should start sneaking around; I'm being blamed for it, anyway!"

"Don't you get smart with me, young lady."

Pauline turned and started back up the stairs. "I gave up being smart with you a long time ago. You never understand."

It was a jab that went over Elizabeth's head. Five minutes later, the ringing of the telephone sent Elizabeth into a rage. "HELLO!" This time the tone of her voice did little to hide her anger.

"Hello, Mrs. Bianchi is—"

"NO, SHE IS NOT! *And if you hoodlums keep calling, I'll talk to your mother!*" Elizabeth enunciated each Italian syllable.

"Mrs. Bianchi? I, I'm sorry to bother you. This is Alonzo, Alonzo Ricci?"

"Oh, my goodness." Elizabeth's nervous laughter was inescapable. "Alonzo, yes, yes, my dear. Did you wish to speak to Pauline?"

"If possible, Mrs. Bianchi. But if this isn't a good time, I can—"

"Oh, yes, yes, my dear. My goodness. I don't know what came over me. I'll let her know you are waiting on the telephone. Pauline? Pauline sweetheart. Alonzo from the church is on the telephone for you."

"Am I allowed to talk to him?" Pauline retorted.

"She'll be right with you, Alonzo. You will forgive me for my outburst. We've had so many pranksters calling and hanging up lately."

Alonzo interrupted, "Mrs. Bianchi, think nothing of it, please. I fully understand."

"Thank you, Alonzo. Oh, here is Pauline. Have a wonderful day, dear. Oh, and do tell your father I'm praying for him as he prepares Sunday's message."

"I'll be sure and let him know, Mrs. Bianchi."

Elizabeth glared at her daughter as she handed Pauline the receiver. This prompted a return glare from Pauline immediately followed by a feigned smile as she jerked the receiver from her mother's hand.

"Hello?" Pauline said with a smile plastered on her face.

"Hey, Pauline," Alonzo said, unfazed by Elizabeth's farce.

"Hey, Alonzo. How are you?"

"I'm lonely. How about that *hot date* over at Bray's? Are you up to it?" Alonzo said jokingly.

"Golly, Alonzo. I'll have to check my datebook. It's been pretty busy lately." Pauline teased.

"What do you say I pick you up in about an hour? We'll chat, get some ice cream, and I will have you back home to argue with your mother by four."

Pauline snickered. She'd never experienced this side of Alonzo and enjoyed his playfulness.

"That sounds great, Alonzo. I'll see you in about an hour. Should I bring my Bible or something?"

Alonzo chuckled, "I think we will be forgiven if we forgo a Bible study this time."

"Okay, see you in about an hour."

"See who in about an hour? Where do you think you're going? You didn't ask." Elizabeth followed Pauline to the foot of the stairs. With her *Woman's Day* in one hand, the other flailing in the air, Elizabeth continued, "See what I mean? Little miss-prissy just comes and goes when she wants without even asking?"

Pauline stepped on the second step of the staircase and turned. She took a deep breath and said matter-of-factly, "Mother. If you wish to tell Alonzo I cannot meet with him, you will have that opportunity when he shows up at the front door in one hour."

A sick expression replaced the sneer on Elizabeth's face. "One hour? What do you mean one hour? Look at this place; look at it! *Non posso credere che mi fai queste cose!* We need to vacuum! We need to straighten up the cushions."

As Pauline continued up the stairs, Elizabeth called out, "Peggy? Peggy, bring the family Bible from Mommy and Daddy's closet. I think it is on the shelf behind the suitcases, sweetheart. Peggy? Did you hear me?"

Pauline continued up the stairs. She had a makeover of her own to tend to. She locked herself in the bathroom. There was no reason not to look her very best—even if it was just a meeting with her youth director.

CHAPTER THIRTY
FOUNTAIN, FAITH, FUTURE
AUGUST 1959

I t only took forty-five minutes for the Bianchi house to appear spotless. The family Bible was conspicuously placed on the coffee table, replacing the *TV Guide*, *True Confessions*, and *Woman's Day* magazines.

One hour after his telephone call, Alonzo knocked on the Bianchi's front door.

Pauline scurried down the stairs to answer it. Alonzo did not expect the door to open so quickly. He'd turned to admire his car parked at the curb. When the door opened, he turned back to Pauline and smiled, "Hi."

It was all he'd said. Perhaps it was the way he said it. Perhaps it was because it was Alonzo Ricci standing at her door. It wasn't Alonzo Ricci, the youth director, but Alonzo Ricci, a friend. Whatever it was, Pauline knew intuitively, something was different. It wasn't just, *hello;* it was, *hi*. In Pauline's mind, it was the kind of *hi* two people say when they first meet and are happy they did. It was apprehensive and yet, anticipatory. Simple, but complex. To anyone else, it might have gone unnoticed, but to Pauline, it was the most wonderful, *hi* she'd ever heard.

"Pauline? Are you okay?"

"Oh, my gosh, Alonzo. Hi—Hello! Come in, come in." As he stepped into the living room, Pauline gushed with nervous chatter. "I'm sorry. I don't know what came over me. Right—hello. So, we've said hello." Pauline nervously paused. "Okay, Hi. Oh, my gosh, I just said it again!"

Alonzo began to laugh. Pauline was charmingly vulnerable.

Pauline continued, "Wanna go get some ice cream—or something?"

"Absolutely! I'm up for a scoop or two," Alonzo replied.

Mrs. Bianchi entered the living room. "Hello, Alonzo. It is so nice of you to call and take some extra time with Pauline."

"Mrs. Bianchi, I'm taking time with all the kids. I think it is important as we prepare for the changes we will be facing in the coming months."

Pauline's heart sank. Alonzo's words slapped her back into reality. She was just another one of the *kids* in the youth group. Another responsibility for Alonzo to take care of before moving on.

"Well, you two have a nice visit. I will see you later, sweetheart." Elizabeth gushed. Pauline turned to offer a replay of her fraudulent smile.

Alonzo opened the car door for Pauline.

"Well, that was a little awkward," Pauline reluctantly said.

"Awkward?" Alonzo chuckled. "Awkward would have been if your mother wanted to join us."

"Oh, my gosh! I don't even want to think about that!"

"Let's get some ice cream. I'm ready for pralines and cream. How about you?"

As they backed out of the Bianchi's driveway Pauline asked, "Alonzo, you're meeting with all the kids? I mean, having ice cream and meeting with all the kids, like we are today?"

A wry smile emerged from Alonzo's lips. "I am meeting with everyone." He looked at her, making sure their eyes met. "And I am doing it after every Sunday evening service."

Pauline couldn't stop the smile that emerged. She gently placed her hand on Alonzo's arm, careful not to interfere with his steering. He quickly glanced in Pauline's direction. Pauline simply smiled and said, "Hi."

"Well, hello," Alonzo replied playfully. "My name is Alonzo Ricci —but you, you can call me Lonnie."

"Lonnie. I like that," Pauline responded.

"It's what my mom and dad call me at home; Lonnie or Lon."

"Why doesn't everyone call you Lonnie?" Pauline asked.

"Nah, it's better when I am in the public eye to go by Alonzo. There's less confusion, and, after all, it is my dad's name. I think Alonzo is more masculine."

"Well, I don't think so. I think it's too formal." Pauline stopped herself from going further. "I'm sorry Alonzo. I didn't mean to imply I don't like your name."

Alonzo blinked and pursed his lips. "Pauline, I didn't take offense. When we are visiting, if you want, you can call me Lonnie. Who knows? I might just begin to like it, too!"

Alonzo parked the car and walked around to open Pauline's door —which she'd already begun to open.

"Hey, wait a minute! Don't all the fellas chasing after you treat you like a lady?" he teased.

"Oh, Alon—," she stopped herself, "Lonnie! I don't have fellas chasing after me."

Alonzo chuckled, "Well if you say so. But if you were to ask me, which I know you didn't, I'd say there are at least a few of them tightening up the shoestrings on their tennis shoes when you are around!"

He fully opened the partially opened door and Pauline stepped out.

"Hello, Alonzo." someone called from across the parking lot.

"Oh, hello, Mrs. Lukins. How are you today?" he shouted back.

"I'm doing very well thank you. And you?" Mrs. Lukins responded.

"I'm doing just great thank you. I'll be doing better when I'm devouring some of Mr. Bray's ice cream!"

"Well, you have a good rest of the week, and we'll see you Sunday," Mrs. Lukins replied. Pauline did not go unnoticed. Mrs. Lukins could not remember her name. "Oh, it's good to see you, dear." Mrs. Lukins politely acknowledged Pauline.

Pauline smiled, "Nice to see you too, ma'am."

As they entered Bray's, Alonzo whispered to Pauline, "That was Mrs. Lukins, from the church."

Pauline responded with surprising firmness, "I know exactly who it is!"

Alonzo straightened himself up and followed her into the pharmacy.

"Hi, kids!" Mr. Bray greeted Alonzo and Pauline as they entered. "What will it be today for you two?"

"Hey, Mr. Bray. I think Pauline and I are prepared to do an Everest all by ourselves!" Alonzo kidded.

"Are there going to be others joining you today?" Mr. Bray asked.

"I hope not," Alonzo replied. His response caught Pauline by surprise. "I promised Pauline a hot date, and that's exactly what I am going to give her!" Alonzo followed his comment with a chuckle leading to Mr. Bray's laughter, followed by an uncomfortable chuckle from Pauline.

Mr. Bray turned to retrieve the day's menu. Pauline nervously whispered, "Is that what this is? Alonzo. Is this a—a date?"

Alonzo turned. "Pauline, we are doing nothing in secret. I promised you we'd go out for a soda sometime, and today is that time. Call it whatever you want to call it. I intend to gorge myself with ice cream and enjoy our time together." A sudden concerned look swept over Alonzo. "Are you uncomfortable?"

Pauline's response was so sudden she blushed. "Uncomfortable? Uncomfortable—no, no not at all. I'm not uncomfortable, Alonzo. Are you?"

Mr. Bray returned with a list of the day's specials.

"Kids, you're in luck. Mrs. Bray has her famous hot fudge on the menu, perfect for a hot date! If you wait a bit, we'll get that ready for you."

Alonzo looked at Pauline and turned to Mr. Bray. "We're in no hurry, no hurry at all. Mrs. Bray's hot fudge sounds terrific. What d'ya say, Paul?"

Pauline smiled at Alonzo. "I say hot fudge sundaes will be great." After Mr. Bray stepped away, Pauline asked, "What did you call me?"

"I don't know. What did I call you?" Alonzo responded.

"You called me Paul; Paul. I kinda liked that. When we are together, you can call me Paul—Lonnie."

Alonzo laughed, "It'll be our secret!"

CHAPTER THIRTY-ONE
BE CAREFUL!
1959

"Hello, sweetheart. How was your day?" Alonzo's mother asked.,

"Hi, Mom. It was a great day! How about yours?" Alonzo replied.

"Oh, it was a very nice day," she responded. "I got a call from Mrs. Lukins this afternoon. She said she saw you at Bray's; said you were with a young lady from the church."

Alonzo's father entered the living room from the kitchen.

"Hi, Lon. How was your day?"

"I was just telling Mom it was a great day. Yours?"

"Every day is a blessing. I finished Sunday's sermon and started getting things together for the upcoming deacon's meeting. What's this I hear about you at Bray's with a young lady from the church?"

"Wow! News gets around fast," Alonzo chuckled. "Yes, I took Pauline Bianchi over to Bray's. We got a hot fudge sundae."

"What was the reason for the meeting?" Alonzo's father asked.

"Reason?" Alonzo asked.

"Yes, what was the reason for the meeting with...? Who did you say it was?"

"Pauline Bianchi," Alonzo replied.

Alonzo's father turned to his wife, "Which one is she?"

"She's Elizabeth's daughter. You know, the pretty girl with the long dark hair," Alonzo's mother replied.

"Ah, yes. Well, I'm more aware of Elizabeth's younger daughter. I only hear about her eldest during prayer meetings. Mrs. Bianchi always requests special prayer for that situation. Seems she's a bit of a problem for the family," Alonzo's father commented.

"Whoa, wait a minute. Pauline is not a situation. I don't think you are hearing the whole story, Dad," Alonzo interrupted.

"What story? I just said her mother has voiced some concerns. What? Am I supposed to ignore what she has said?"

"No, not necessarily ignore it, but I hope you would recognize there are two sides to every story. As you said, you don't even know Pauline," Alonzo explained.

"Lon, let me tell you something. You are a young man; a good-looking young man. In the ministry, you have to be very careful. You can't afford to even appear to have favorites. Keep a distance. It's not unusual for these young girls to get a crush on a fella like you. You make sure you don't encourage them."

"Dad, we got a sundae—in the afternoon—in broad daylight—at Bray's—in front of God—and all creation!"

"Just make sure it doesn't happen again. I think Mrs. Lukins was a little concerned about appearances, and she has every right to be. I'm glad she called and told your mom." Alonzo's father leaned forward to emphasize the importance of his comment. "You are being scrutinized. As unfair as it might seem to you right now, you, your mother, and all of us are under a microscope. Be careful, son. Be careful."

Alonzo could not contain his exasperation. "Well, as long as we are praising Mrs. Lukins, for her *meddling ministry,* I'll share what I think. I think she is a snoopy gossip who has no business sticking her nose in my business!" Alonzo continued. "What? Did she miss her afternoon soap opera? Did she have to make up for it with her own drama? This is ridiculous! We are talking about an ice cream sundae, Dad!"

"You've got a lot of growing up to do young man. A lot! You've only got a short time before heading off to school." Alonzo's father pointed his finger directly at Alonzo. "Don't make any foolish mistakes now."

The discussion was over. Alonzo stomped toward the hall that led to his room. His father called out to him once again, "And put an end to these private meetings."

In his room, Alonzo thought to himself, *oh, yeah, it was a great day, a great day.*

CHAPTER THIRTY-TWO
PAULINE'S CONFUSION
1959

Intuitively, Pauline realized she had to suppress a growing emotional attachment to Alonzo, but she couldn't get him out of her mind. The more she thought about him, the more she wrestled with the lingering fear Alonzo's interest was a figment of her overstimulated, teenage imagination. Perhaps, she'd put him in an awkward situation. Perhaps, she was unwittingly orchestrating a self-satisfying manipulation for his attention. Who would do such a thing? He'd been so kind; such a gentleman. Who would...?

Pauline was horrified by the answer to her musings. Her mother! Her mother would surreptitiously do anything to get what she wanted! The thought was repulsive. So repulsive was Pauline's self-evaluation she vowed to avoid Alonzo at all costs. A heavy, dark sense of guilt weighed heavy upon Pauline's shoulders. How could she have been so foolish? No, no, Pauline had to end what she'd convinced herself would ultimately be an embarrassing unrequited interest anyway.

The next morning the Bianchi's telephone rang. Pauline just happened to be sitting in the kitchen and answered it.

"Hello?"

"Oh, Hi Pauline. I'm glad you answered the telephone. It's Lonnie," Alonzo chuckled.

Pauline swallowed hard. *Why did I answer the phone?*

"Oh, hello, Alonzo." Her monotone response did not go unnoticed.

"Is everything all right?" Alonzo asked.

"All right? Sure, yeah, everything is all right." Pauline's mind was scurrying for something to say. Something that would gracefully end the conversation. The longer she took to gather her thoughts, the less controllable her resentment for Alonzo's call.

"What is it you want? I mean, why are you calling?" As the words burst from her lips, she realized how terse her response sounded.

"I was just calling to thank you for getting together with me yesterday. I want you to know how much I enjoyed it." Alonzo paused. "I hope we can do it again sometime."

Even though Alonzo's words were well intended, they intensified Pauline's emotional struggle. Was she fooling herself? Was she hearing what she wanted to hear, or was it possible Alonzo Ricci, Jr. had an interest in her?

The situation was unbearable. Pauline was caught off guard by Alonzo's telephone call. She was confused about his intentions and not willing to torture herself any further by the sound of his voice. "Yeah, it was fun. It was a nice time, Alonzo. Thank you."

There was a moment of silence.

Pauline then responded to Alonzo's offer. "Yeah, yeah sure—sure. Maybe we'll do it again sometime. Hey, look, I'm sorry, Alonzo, but I've got to go. I've got a lot of things I've got to do today. But thank you for calling. Yeah, uh, yeah, thanks for the call; bye."

Alonzo sat at his desk with the receiver still in his hand; a deafening dial tone blared in his ear.

Maybe Dad was right.

CHAPTER THIRTY-THREE
JERRY PENNYPACKER
1959

"Hi, Mrs. Pennypacker? This is Pauline, Pauline Bianchi. Is Jerry available?"

"Hi, Pauline. How is your mother?"

"Oh, she's fine. Is Jerry available?"

"Oh, that's good. She is such a wonderful lady. You are very lucky to have her as your mother," Mrs. Pennypacker gushed.

"Oh, well," Pauline paused to think of an appropriate response. "She is certainly loved by a lot of people."

"She certainly is. How are your sister and father?"

"Oh, they are fine, fine. Mrs. Pennypacker can I—"

"Do you ever think we'll see your father at church? So many people are praying for him."

"Well, you never know. Can I speak with Jerry please?" Pauline blurted.

"Oh, why certainly. Just a moment, dear."

Pauline took a deep breath; *finally!*

"Jerold; Jerold? Pauline Bianchi is on the telephone for you. Jerold?" Mrs. Pennypacker returned to the telephone. "Just a moment, dear. He will be right down. So, is there something going on with the youth group this weekend?"

Pauline thought for a moment. There was nothing she was aware of. "Nothing I can think of, Mrs. Pennypacker," Pauline replied.

"Oh, well. I just thought you might be calling about a special activity or something."

Pauline realized Mrs. Pennypacker was fishing for information, not that there was anything to divulge, but the realization Mrs. Pennypacker was fishing created a sense of momentary satisfaction.

Pauline giggled. *Or something*, she thought.

"Here's Jerry, dear. Please tell your mother I said hello."

"I will remember to tell her, Mrs. Pennypacker." Pauline was relieved when she handed the phone over to Jerry.

"Hello?" Jerry's upbeat voice filled the receiver.

"Hi, Jerry. It's Pauline."

"I know WHO it is, what I want to know is WHY you would be calling me," Jerry responded.

"You, goof! I just wanted to call and see how you are. We haven't had much time together and I've missed talking to you," Pauline said.

"Well, I'm okay. There's not much to tell you. Everything is fine. What about you?"

"Me? I'm okay too. Let's see, my mother drives me crazy, my father is invisible, my sister is perfect—everything is fine," Pauline sarcastically responded.

"Sounds like maybe you could use a friend," Jerry coyly offered.

"Sure could—*friend*. Wanna get together?"

"You know I do. When? What do you wanna do? Where should we meet? Can I pick you up?" Jerry blabbered uncontrollably.

Pauline giggled. "Any place other than Bray's would be great," Pauline said.

"Is there something wrong with Bray's?" Jerry asked.

Pauline's giggling stopped. She immediately felt a surge of frustration. Why was Jerold Pennypacker questioning her? *Did he want to get together or not?*

"Does there have to be something wrong with Bray's?" Pauline retorted. "Jerry, there's nothing wrong with Bray's. It's just, it's just," Pauline took a deep breath. "Jerry, it's just too busy. We haven't talked for, I don't know—how many weeks has it been? If we go to Mr. Bray's we'll be lucky to say *hello* without someone from the neighborhood interrupting."

"Pauline, you name the place. It's fine with me."

"Why don't we just go to the park?" Pauline suggested.

The suggestion was appealing to Jerry, surprising, but appealing.

"The park. Okay, the park. Which park do you wanna go to?

"Any park. I just want to get together. You think of a park. Do I have to do everything?" Pauline spouted.

Jerry laughed. "Okay, okay. I'll think of a park, no problem. Let's save the arguing for when we get together. It will give us something to do."

"I'm sorry, Jerry. I didn't want to argue. I just called to see if you would like to get together, that's all."

"Well, we've crossed that bridge. When would you like to go to the park? I suggest we do it as soon as possible—before you change your mind," Jerry laughed.

"Oh, Jerold Pennypacker! Don't be silly!" Pauline returned the chuckle. "How about I put together a picnic basket and we go this afternoon?"

"That sounds terrific! I've got a few things to do this morning, but I could pick you up around noon. Would that work for you?"

"Noon sounds perfect! What do you want in the picnic basket?" Pauline asked.

"I don't care. Food! I'm sure anything you put together will be perfect," Jerry replied.

"Well then, what do you want to drink?" Pauline asked.

"I'll pick up a couple of 7-Ups if that's okay with you," Jerry offered.

"That'll be great. See you at noon."

"If you change your mind, I'm still coming over for the picnic basket," Jerry teased.

"You goof. I'll see you at noon." Pauline hung up the telephone. Perhaps a picnic with Jerry would help her repress any irrational thoughts of Alonzo.

Jerry arrived shortly before noon.

"So, where we goin'?" Pauline asked.

"Ya know, I thought for kicks we could go over to Little Park by the airfield. It's kinda neat watching the planes come and go," Jerry replied.

"The airfield?" Pauline responded.

"Sure! Unless you've got a better idea."

Pauline thought about it. The old Jamesburg airfield park might be the perfect getaway. "I think it's a great idea. Let's get going," Pauline replied.

The old Jamesburg Airfield was established in the 1930s. Many of the more affluent Monroe Township citizens owned their own airplanes and would use the field as a home base for business and recreation. Rumor was it soon would be demolished, and the adjacent park would be expanded. For now, other than the occasional roar of an incoming or outgoing airplane, the present park was secluded and quiet. Jerry thought it was just the place to reestablish his relationship with Pauline.

It was a twenty-minute drive to the airfield. Jerry pulled off the road and onto what appeared to be a maintenance entry. The entrance had not been used for years. He parked the car in front of the barrier, walked around the back of the car, and opened Pauline's door.

"Why, thank you, kind sir," Pauline said as she held out her hand for Jerry's assistance.

"Think nothing of it, fair maiden," Jerry replied.

Pauline laughed. "My dad used to call me that when I was a little girl. I was his princess, and he was my knight in shining armor."

Pauline then scoffed. "My mother has always been the wicked witch."

"Well, let's not bring her to the picnic," Jerry wisely advised. "I'll get the basket if you'd get the blanket."

The two made their way around the rusty barrier. There was a trail post just on the other side.

"It's this way," Jerry pointed.

"What's this way?" Pauline asked.

"Through the grove. Come on; you'll see." Jerry led the way.

The old, gnarled oaks looked as if they'd stood sentinel since the beginning of time, venerable guardians of what lie ahead.

"Come on, Pauline," Jerry called back to Pauline, who trailed behind, enjoying the sun's rays through the broad, moss-covered timbers.

"I'm coming, I'm coming." Pauline watched as Jerry momentarily disappeared behind a grouping of the thickest of enormous oaks. "Slow down, will ya?" Pauline called out.

Jerry laughed, "Get a hitch in it, girl. You're almost here."

Pauline followed the trail around the large grouping of oaks onto a spacious meadow of wildflowers. Black-eyed Susans stood outside the rows of oaks, framing purple coneflowers, American bellflowers, and a sea of butterfly weed. The meadow itself sloped onto a fairway of deep blue-green perennial ryegrass.

"Let's lay the blanket right here," Jerry advised. "We'll get the best view from here."

As Pauline flattened out the blanket, a plane flew directly overhead.

"Whoa! That was awesome Jerry," Pauline said. "How did you find out about this place?"

"My uncle told me about it. He comes here often," Jerry replied.

"Well, you can't get much closer to the airplanes without being in the cockpit," Pauline teased as she took the picnic basket from Jerry.

At the other end of the meadow, a plane was preparing to take off.

"Why don't we wait just a bit before we eat," Jerry suggested.

Pauline sat down on the blanket and placed the basket beside her. She patted the blanket. "Come on Jerry. Sit down." Jerry seemed to ignore her as he raised his hand to his forehead to shield the sun from his eyes.

"Come on, Jerry. What? You waiting for a flight?" she teased.

The roar of the old biplane engines increased as the plane made its way down the runway.

"That thing is never going to get off the ground unless it speeds up!" Pauline shouted over the oncoming engine. Jerry just laughed.

Pauline shielded her eyes and watched as the wildflowers leaned toward the oaks with the rush of air from the oncoming airplane. Jerry stood on his tiptoes, waving to the pilot.

The pilot cut back the throttle of the beautiful red biplane as it came to rest just in front of Jerry and Pauline. He pulled his goggles up and onto his forehead.

"Hey, Jerry! How are you doing, pal?" The pilot shouted.

"I'm doing great, Uncle Warren! How about you?" Jerry shouted back.

Uncle Warren? Pauline thought.

"The two of you ready for a ride?" Uncle Warren asked, still shouting over the whirling propeller.

"Jerry! A ride? In an airplane? IN A BIPLANE? Are you kidding me?" Pauline took a deep breath. "Jerry, WHAT DID YOU DO?"

Jerry just started laughing. "You left the planning up to me. What d'ya think—you in?"

"Are you kidding me? Of course, I am in. Oh, my goodness! Jerry, Jerold Pennypacker! Are you kidding me?" Pauline was overcome with excitement.

"You kids get in the front. I've got goggles up there for you. Don't smile too much or you'll get a mouth full of bugs," Uncle Warren laughed. "Young lady, do you have something to keep your hair from flying around?"

"I've got some bands," Pauline shouted.

"I'm sorry," Jerry said. "Uncle Warren, this is Pauline. Pauline, this is my Uncle Warren."

"It's a real pleasure to meet you, Pauline. This is my second time flying, so it will be nice to have some company up there this time," he teased.

"Well, it's my first," Pauline shouted as Uncle Warren increased the engine power and released the left brake turning the plane to face the runway.

"Hold on tight, kids! Let's take this baby to the skies where she belongs."

Pauline grabbed hold of Jerry's hand as the plane bumped over the grassy runway and then effortlessly lifted into the sky. Pauline felt the wind pulling at her cheeks as the plane banked to the left, leaving behind the oak grove and the airfield. As it flew over Buckelew Avenue, Pauline could smell the butterscotch from Kerr's butterscotch factory.

"Oh, Jerry. This is magical; this is magical!" Pauline shouted.

Jerry's smile stretched from ear to ear. Never mind the bugs, the smile could not be erased from his face.

"So, ya like it?" Jerry asked.

Pauline tightened her grip on Jerry's hand. "Like it? Oh, Jerry. I love it. This is the best picnic ever—the best day ever!"

"Pauline? How ya doing up there?" Uncle Warren shouted.

"I'm about to flip my lid, Uncle Warren!" Pauline screamed with excitement.

"Well, get ready because we are about to do just that!" Uncle Warren shouted.

With that, Uncle Warren pulled back on the yoke sending the nose of the plane upward. The barrel loop maneuver was over before Pauline had a chance to prepare herself.

"What d'ya think, Pauline?" Uncle Warren shouted.

"Can we do it again?" Pauline shouted back to Uncle Warren.

"Absolutely! Hold on tight," Uncle Warren advised as he once again began the aerial maneuver.

The trio flew over Monroe Township, Englishtown, Morganville, and South Brunswick before returning to the airfield. All in all, it was a one-hour, fun-filled excursion. The plane landed on the grassy runway and rolled up to Pauline's and Jerry's picnic area.

"Okay, kids! Thanks a bundle for keeping me company up there," Uncle Warren casually said.

"Oh, my gosh. Thank you! That was the best time of my life!" Pauline exclaimed.

"You are a great passenger. We'll do it again sometime, Pauline. You are a natural."

Jerry helped Pauline out of her front left seat, onto the wing, and the ground. They both turned and waved as Uncle Warren revved up the engine and once again made his way down the runway and into the sky.

Pauline abruptly hugged Jerry and gave him a kiss. "Jerry, thank you. This is the best day of my life!"

Jerry touched the side of his lip where their lips had just met. "Golly, Pauline. Had I known you'd be this excited, I'd taken you up there years ago."

Pauline slapped him on the shoulder. "Silly."

They walked back to their picnic area. The blanket had rolled over the basket from the thrust of the plane's propeller. Fortunately, the basket remained closed although it had flipped onto its side.

"Jerry, I've made Black Hawk sliced Thuringer, pickled pimento loaf, and chopped ham sandwiches for us. There's Mr. Mustard and pickles if you'd like. Oh, and Saratoga chips. For dessert, we've got Rice Krispies treats. I hope it's okay." Pauline said. "But nothing will live up to what you have done. Thank you." Again, Pauline gently kissed Jerry—this time on the cheek.

"Well, that's it! I just had my dessert!" Jerry jokingly said. "Let's break into that basket!"

CHAPTER THIRTY-FOUR
MARC'S CALL
1959

At four o'clock the telephone rang. It rang once, then twice. It stopped ringing just before Mrs. Bianchi could pick up the receiver.

"*I hate that telefono!*" She muttered as she slammed the receiver back onto its carriage.

A short time later, Pauline picked up the receiver and dialed.

"Who are you calling?" Elizabeth asked.

"I'm calling Marc Romano, Mother."

"That isn't appropriate! A young lady does not call a young man." Elizabeth crossed her arms in her usual disapproving fashion.

"Thank you, Mother. I'm going to call him and give him that information."

"Hello?" Marc answered the phone.

"Hi, Marc. It's Pauline."

"Thank you for calling back. I've been trying to reach you, but I'm having trouble getting past your mother." Marc's voice didn't mask his frustration.

"Yea, I know. I'm sorry. How have you been?" Pauline asked.

"Me? I've been great. You?"

"Oh, I'm fine, fine." Pauline then added, "I've missed talking to you." *Where did that come from?* Pauline thought to herself.

"Yea, that's why I called. I've missed talking with you too. Wanna get together or something?"

"I'd love to. What do you have in mind?"

"Well, there's always Bray's." Marc knew the suggestion would get under Pauline's skin.

"Marc, so help me if you are serious," Pauline caught herself when she realized Marc was just kidding. "Don't get me wrong, but I'm not comfortable going to Bray's. Too many nosey people and loose lips around this neighborhood. Besides, the same place gets old. Wanna try something new?"

"Sure! What do you have in mind?"

"Do you skate?" Pauline hinted.

"Nah, not something I've gotten the hang of. I spend enough time on my butt playing football."

"Let's go to Pocono Rollerama then. I'm going to give you some competition, Mr. Romano."

"Should I pick you up at your house?" Marc asked with a bit of trepidation in his throat.

"I think it would be better if you pick me up at Gatzmer's. I'll walk over there to meet you."

"Okay. Meet in about an hour?"

"One hour will be great! I can't wait to see you." Pauline said.

"Me too."

Pauline met Marc at Gatzmer's. Marc then drove the fifteen miles to Pocono Rollerama.

Pocono's was built in 1948. It was the local hangout for teens since that time. Pauline felt far enough away from First Reliance to relax and have a good time. Marc soon discovered he'd been bamboozled; Pauline was an accomplished skater.

As he carefully held onto the inner rink wall, Pauline walked onto the floor without the slightest hesitation. "Come on, silly! You're the athlete!" Pauline giggled.

"And I want to continue to be an athlete without breaking my neck on these crazy skates," Marc replied. "Why did I let you talk me into this?"

Pauline reached out both hands and encouraged Marc to skate with her.

"Let me make it around once on my own before I take the chance of killing us both," Marc joked.

"Okay!"

With that, Pauline effortlessly skated into the myriad of skaters. She lapped everyone on the floor while comfortably performing crossovers and grapevines. Then, without any break in her speed, she immediately swiveled, skating backward into a backward cross.

While Pauline continued to put on a show, Marc had become the star attraction to a five-year-old girl who giggled hysterically. His legs also skated effortlessly—in every direction imaginable.

"Got the hang of it yet?" Pauline asked as she passed Marc for a third time.

"Oh, sure, sure. I'm almost ready for the Jersey Jolters," Marc responded sarcastically.

Pauline flowed into a salchow and final spin before exiting across the flow of skaters to Marc.

"Well, what do you think?" Pauline asked.

"Can't think of a time when I've had more fun," Marc replied. "No, wait a minute. There was that time in elementary school when I fell off the monkey bars and broke my arm..."

Pauline ignored his sarcasm. "Looks to me like you've progressed about eight feet; that's good. Have you tried to let go of the wall yet?" Pauline kidded.

Marc had to laugh at himself and the situation he was in. By this time, the little girl had gathered the rest of her friends to watch.

"Come on, Marc. Trust me." Pauline once again held out her hands for Marc to take hold.

"I will go very slowly, promise. You just hold on and let me pull you around. When you feel comfortable, you can try lifting your feet and pushing off to the sides."

"Okay, coach! I'm in your hands." Marc stumbled away from the wall and held onto Pauline's hands.

The lights dimmed as a melodic voice came over the public address system, "Alright, skaters. The next song is couples only; couples only skate."

Pauline continued to pull Marc as couples sped past them.

"Don't worry about them. You just keep your eye on me, and let me pull you," Pauline instructed.

"I'm not worried about them. I'm worried about you. You're the one who got me into this mess in the first place." Marc smiled uncomfortably.

Pauline laughed.

Marc attempted to pick up his right skate. The sudden change in tempo caused him to lurch forward in an uncontrollable run toward Pauline. The two collided and landed on the wooden rink floor.

Marc and Pauline sat, laughing too hard to get up. Marc never let go of Pauline's hands. Without warning, Marc pulled her close and kissed her.

Pauline pulled away in shock. "What was that?"

"Well, if I'm not mistaken, it was a kiss," Marc replied.

"But... but why? Why did you kiss me?" a confused Pauline asked.

"Because you were the one holding my hands. I couldn't think of anything else to do. It just seemed right," Marc very calmly responded.

"Well, well, it wasn't. It wasn't the right thing to do. I mean— here, in front of everyone," Pauline stammered.

"Should it have been somewhere else?" Marc inquired.

"Yes. I mean, no! I mean... I don't know what I mean. You just surprised me, that's all. I mean, it was so sudden, so fast. I didn't even get a chance to know I was being kissed! There was no warn-ing," Pauline continued to stammer.

"Would you rather I warn you from now on?" Marc asked as he leaned forward for an encore performance.

"No! I mean, maybe; I don't know! Marc, you were the one who said we had to be careful; we had to meet on the sly," Pauline argued.

"Yes, I did." Marc looked at the couples skating around them and the skaters standing outside the wall, awaiting their chance to resume skating.

"Do you know anyone here?" he asked.

"Well, no. I—"

Marc held up his hand to silence her. "Neither do I. I think we're pretty safe, Pauline."

"Well, we are not very safe sitting right here in the middle of the floor," Pauline chided. "Let's get over to the side before we get trampled."

Back in the seats lining the perimeter of the rink, Pauline unlaced her skates.

"Hey, what d'ya doing? I was just starting to like this sport," Marc joked.

"I bet you were," Pauline replied, knowing it was not the skating he was referring to.

"Come on, Pauline. Give me another chance. I promise to be a good student."

"Okay, Romano. But I'm putting you on probation."

"Warning understood, coach," Marc replied as he saluted.

Pauline remained stern. However, Pauline struggled to relive the feeling of his kiss. It just happened too quickly.

CHAPTER THIRTY-FIVE

TURNING THE PAIGE
1959

"Hello, Mrs. Bianchi. I need to talk to Pauline."

Knowing perfectly well it was Paige, Elizabeth asked, "And whom shall I say is calling?"

"Why don't you tell her it's Marc Romano," Paige replied.

Paige's stern response took Elizabeth by surprise.

"Pauline," she paused as she considered divulging Paige's flippant suggestion. She decided otherwise. "Paige is on the telephone." Elizabeth covered the receiver as Pauline entered the kitchen. "What did you do to her? She sounds upset. Paige is a nice girl and your best friend. You better not be—"

"Thank you, Mother. I'm very well aware of who Paige is. Please let me have the telephone."

"Hi, Paige. What's cook'n?"

"That's what I'd like to know, Pauline. Are you and Marc seeing each other?"

Without hesitation, Pauline responded, "Yes. Yes, we are seeing each other at church, at school, and sometimes in the neighborhood; yes, we are most definitely seeing each other."

"Come on, Pauline. You know what I mean," Paige insisted.

"Yes, Paige. Yes, I do, and frankly, I wish you didn't feel you had to ask. I am not going to do anything to jeopardize our friendship. Marc's a swell guy, but I'm not interested."

"Well, I see the way he looks at you."

"And that's my fault?"

"I don't see you doing anything about it," Paige continued.

Pauline quickly surmised it was time to take control of the conversation. "And what would you suggest I do? Stop attending the youth group? Change schools? Come on—be serious! Paige, it's me, Pauline. You know I wouldn't do anything to hurt you. Why would you ever suggest such a thing? That's not fair, Paige. That's not fair at all, and it hurts that you would question my friendship."

"Well, I... I wasn't sure. Well, I mean I know you wouldn't, but I wasn't sure if he was chasing you and what you were doing about it —if he was, I mean—if he was, and, if you weren't; it's just that—"

"Paige! Stop. Listen to yourself. You're not making any sense. Nothing is going on between Marc and me. Nothing is going on between Jerry and me. We are all just friends—and you are my closest friend. Remember?"

"I'm sorry. It's just, Marc never pays attention to me. He never calls—he never does anything," Paige lamented.

"Maybe you need to stop waiting for him to make the first move and start acting on your own," Pauline suggested. "Help him along a little, girl."

"But I want him to chase after me on his own. I don't want to chase him," Paige explained.

"That's just silly. You're being too proud. I'm sorry, but it's the truth, Paige. If you want him to take an interest in you, let him know you are interested and available," Pauline advised.

"How do I do that?"

"Do you have to ask? Really? Paige, talk to him. Sit by him in church. Bake another apple pie if you have to. You tell everyone else he's your guy. Marc's the only one who doesn't know about it."

"Okay, okay. I'm sorry. I'm sorry I suspected you." Paige sheepishly asked, "Sisters?"

"Sisters always," Pauline emphatically responded.

"Okay. Thank you, Pauline. I'm, I'm sorry I suspected anything."

Pauline hung up the telephone and immediately called Marc. She let the telephone ring once, twice, and then she hung up. Almost immediately, the Bianchi's telephone rang.

Knowing it was Marc, responding to their code Pauline answered, "Hi, got a minute?"

"Sure. Is there something wrong?" Marc asked.

"It's Paige. Marc, Paige really likes you. She just called me and was very upset. She blamed me for chasing after you. Well, she blamed me for not stopping you from chasing after me."

Marc chuckled and asked, "And how are you supposed to do that?"

"Come on, Marc. I'm not joking—this is serious. Paige is my best friend. I've told you I do not want to hurt her."

"Pauline, don't get me wrong. Paige seems to be a nice girl, but she's never indicated to me she likes me."

"Yeah, I told her that."

"You what?" Marc sounded startled.

"I told her she should make the first move. You know, open up a little."

"Ha! Tell her to bake another apple pie." Marc mocked.

"I told her that too," Pauline responded.

Marc laughed. Diverting the discussion from being about Paige, Marc continued. "Besides, I'm kind of interested in someone else."

"Marc!" Pauline scolded.

"Pauline... look, I know you are at least a little interested in me. I'll tell ya what. I'm not going to do anything different. We'll be careful, just like we planned. We'll be even more careful if we have to. I like getting together with you."

"Marc, you haven't paid attention to a word I've said!" Pauline attempted to break through his obstinance, but it wasn't working.

"All right then, tell me you don't want to get together. Tell me you want me to stop calling you. Tell me you haven't enjoyed our time together. Tell me you are tired of me, and you want me to leave you alone. Tell me you never think about what happened at Pocono's the other day. Go ahead, tell me. I'm waiting."

Pauline didn't know how to respond. Was there an attraction? Sure, there was. Did she like being pursued? Certainly. Was she willing to tell Marc to stop calling? No, but she couldn't just come out and tell him. "Marc, that's not fair. I'm not going to tell you I'm tired of you or that I want you to leave me alone. I just, I just... I just want there to not be a problem."

"And that's why we are being careful," Marc concluded.

"Marc, I've got to go. I just want to be careful. I don't want anyone to get hurt."

"I've heard you say that a couple of times now. All right, I get it! No one needs to be hurt." For a moment, their breaths synchronized over the line before Marc said, "You worry too much."

"Maybe I do. Anyway, gotta go. Toodle-oo," Pauline said. She hung the phone up and hung her head, but a sneaky grin made it to her lips.

CHAPTER THIRTY-SIX
CASUAL MEETING

1959

Alonzo put the finishing touches on his Sunday evening devotional when the telephone rang. "Good afternoon. Thank you for calling First Reliance Baptist Church. This is Alonzo Ricci. How can I help you?"

"Lon, it's Dad. Your mother and I have a few hospital calls to make this afternoon. I haven't taken the bundled papers to Higgins yet. Could you get that done for me? We should be back around six-thirty this evening."

Higgins Disposal was located in Franklin Township, about forty-five minutes south of Monroe Township. The business was very generous to organizations that collected and returned local newspapers.

"Sure, Dad. I can do that," Alonzo said.

"Great! Great! Listen, there's some leftover pizza in the refrigerator. You can have that for lunch if you want."

"Okay, Dad. I'll see you later tonight." Alonzo hung up the telephone. Pauline stood in the doorway.

"Pauline! What brings you over here?" Alonzo jerked a little in his seat at the sight of her.

"You do, silly! I just came by to see what you were up to. Am I interrupting you?"

"No, no. I was just finishing Sunday evening's devotional." Alonzo got up from his desk and walked over to Pauline. "Come on in. You're not interrupting anything. I'm glad you came over."

Pauline stepped into Alonzo's office and sat on the old couch as Alonzo closed the door.

CHAPTER THIRTY-SEVEN
THE ENVELOPE
1959

Howard Kurdzuk seemed to appear out of nowhere. He approached Pauline from behind, fully intending to startle her. Reaching around her right shoulder, he flipped a sealed offering envelope in front of her face. The envelope bore her name.

"Excuse me, young lady. I believe this is for you." His voice was as harsh as his features. "It was pinned to the usher's board. I'd prefer you and your friends not use the usher's board to pass your notes."

Pauline reached out to take the envelope, but Mr. Kurdzuk pulled it back. Howard was a man to avoid. He stood over six feet. He was an imposing figure to the high school youth at First Reliance Baptist Church. His thick forearms were overdeveloped from years of heavy construction. He'd retained a thick, wavy silver head of hair which was accentuated by his dark leathery skin. His jaw jutted forward and slightly to the right. Even when he was happy, he had the appearance of a sinister bulldog.

Pauline shivered as Mr. Kurdzuk took her arm and led her toward the front of the church. She could feel her pulse under the grip of his fingers.

Pauline quietly spoke, "I'd prefer to sit a little further back if you don't mind."

His jaw remained clenched. Only his lips moved as he whispered back authoritatively, "I do mind. You young people need to be sitting up front, paying attention—not sitting in the back, passing notes and carrying on."

Pauline took the sealed offering envelope from him and sat in full view of his watchful eye.

Pastor Al's message was a blur. All Pauline could think about was the sealed offering envelope Mr. Kurdzuk had given to her.

Forty-five minutes later, Pastor Al finished his message, and Irene McCarthy softly played the third stanza of "Just As I Am." It was always the altar call, and Pastor Al always asked Irene to play one more time while the choir quietly sang the third stanza.

Pauline thought Pastor Al missed his real calling—theater. His oratory pattern was carefully choreographed. He slowly leaned forward over the lectern and glanced from side to side as if to make certain the intended prey, his congregation, was not also being stalked by the adversary, Satan himself. Even though it was just a whisper, his melodic voice would lull the congregation into a catatonic mindset—willing and open to receive the full burst of power when his whispers transformed into impassioned cries to yield to the Spirit. Without warning, he would thrust both arms forward, his upward begging hands grotesquely shaking, pleading with the listening hearts of the congregation. A large vein in his forehead would protrude as the sweat would roll down the sides of his brow. His jaw clenched, his reddened face contorted, swelling with emotion. The veins in his neck pulsated as he threw his head back and his eyes opened wide as if to stare directly into heaven itself.

His lips would part and he would admonish the congregation to, "REPENT! REPENT! OH, CAN YOU HEAR THE VOICE OF JESUS CALLING? LISTEN. LISTEN!"

He dropped his head in total exhaustion, hands clinging to either side of the lectern, and his body slowly, ever so slightly swayed—

quietly. There would not be a sound. Even the sounds of the settling wooden church dared not creak as the echo of his pleas filled the room.

Pastor Al, panted as if he'd just finished a marathon, breaking the silence. He punctuated every point with staccato accuracy. "I - want - every - head - bowed! Every eye closed! Choir sing it; sing the next verse like you've never sung it before!"

Pauline's head bowed. She could feel the penetrating eyes of Howard Kurdzuk burn through the back of her skull as he watched her every move. Her long black hair tumbled forward, hiding her face. Quietly, she stared at the envelope, eager to read its contents.

"I want absolute silence," Pastor Al leaned further forward, whispering into the pulpit microphone. "Shhhh." His shushing tapered off into silence, a long, uncomfortable silence.

The silence was broken by the intensity of his dyspneic whisper. "There is still someone here who needs to hear God's voice, and I don't want anything to interrupt His call."

Great; whoever it is, get right with God, and get it over with, will ya? thought Pauline as she struggled to quietly open the sealed offering envelope. She slid her fingernail under the small opening on the side, but her slightest attempt resulted in a crinkling sound she was certain Howard Kurdzuk could hear.

All was quiet—except for the footsteps. Pauline heard them slowly walking up the aisle toward the pew where she was seated. Panic set in. Had he heard? Was he coming? She froze, tightly gripping the envelope. She was prepared to bolt from the pew, out the side door, and into the night. The footsteps continued toward Pauline and slowed to a stop as they arrived directly next to her—but only for a moment. Pauline raised her eyes just enough to catch sight of Deacon Remington as he passed Pauline to the front of the church where several parishioners were kneeling. Pauline took a deep breath. She gasped as if it was the first breath she had taken in hours. Her body trembled as the air filled her lungs.

"Lord, we thank you for your call, we thank you for yet another chance to fully enjoy a relationship with you. Thank you to those who have come, and who have heeded your call. We pray for them, Lord. We pray that they hear your voice and feel your presence in the days, months, and years to come. We pray all these things in Jesus's name," Pastor Ricci smiled. It was broad and inviting. With his arms spread wide, he looked at the congregation. "And the congregation said?"

In unison, the congregation shouted, "Amen!"

The only thing separating Pauline from the contents of the envelope was the offering.

"Ladies and gentlemen, it's been a good day and a great evening of fellowship. Amen?"

In unison, the congregation once again shouted back, "Amen!"

Pastor Al continued, "It's been a victorious day! Amen?"

The congregation more boisterously shouted back, "AMEN!"

Ilene McCarthy was ready for her cue. Pastor Al echoed their approval, "Amen!"

Irene began playing the introduction to "Victory In Jesus!" It was a rousing hymn that, when blended with the drama of the altar call, roused the congregation to reach deep into their billfolds for the offering.

Pastor Al continued, "Let's give back to God with thanksgiving! Don't give until it hurts; give until it feels good! Amen?"

There were noticeably fewer "Amens." Most were replaced by a smattering of quiet, guilty chuckles.

As the offering plate passed by, individual members in the row would stand. There was nothing private or inconspicuous about the taking of the offering. It was not meant to be a spectator portion of the service; everyone saw everyone give.

Pauline was seated on the first seat in the third pew from the front—right next to the aisle. The envelope she had been given was in her right hand while both hands supported her open hymnal. She'd become so focused on the realization the service was almost over she didn't notice the first time the wooden plate tapped her arm. It tapped her arm once again. Pauline looked to her left and up into the eyes of Howard Kurdzuk. He stood, staring at the crinkled envelope in Pauline's hand. With a quick but firm nod, he motioned Pauline to drop the envelope on the offering plate. Pauline's emotions went from fear to rage. She deliberately but quietly set the hymnal in her lap, and without warning she grabbed the offering plate from Howard Kurdzuk's hands. She passed it down to the person on her right, then turned back to Howard, whose menacing glare was met by a rare but equally determined glare from Pauline. Their eyes remained locked on each other. Unflinching, Pauline stood with the rest of the congregation singing, "Victory In Jesus!" Her eyes never left his. This was one battle she knew she would win. Howard was forced to break free from their stares and move to the next row. Pauline smiled, held the envelope in front of her, and broke its seal. She made certain Mr. Kurdzuk was aware of what she was doing; she taunted him.

The service ended with prayer. Pauline quickly made her way from the pew and through the side exit door; the door that was for emergencies. It was her emergency escape from Howard Kurdzuk. She walked briskly across the parking lot, up Gatzmer Avenue and toward Harrison Street. Crossing Harrison, Pauline ducked into Gatzmer Grocers and opened the envelope.

"8:45; Same place. I'll pick you up. We must be careful!"

She waited behind the bus stop—out of sight. She'd arrived only moments before her rendezvous was to take place. Hidden from the overhead streetlight, Pauline waited for the flashing headlamps of his car.

The minutes seemed like hours. He'd never been late before. He would never leave her in the darkness alone. Something must have happened. Pauline stepped out of the shadows and quickly began to walk back to the church parking lot. She was only a few steps away from the lot when the flashing light startled her. She ran toward the car. While hope filled her heart, she quickly realized this was not the car she had been waiting for.

"Hey Pauline, watcha doing out here?" the male voice inquired.

The car's bright headlamps hid the driver from Pauline's view. She knew immediately it was not his voice. Slowing her pace, she hesitantly walked toward the car. The driver leaned over the passenger side of the car, reaching for the door handle.

"Oh, my gosh. Hi, Mr. Hutto. I didn't realize it was you."

"Can I give you a ride home?"

"Uh, well, I... I thought I had a ride, but it doesn't seem to be coming."

"Well, all right then. Hop in and we'll get you home."

"It's only a couple of blocks. I'll be okay."

"Nonsense. You shouldn't be by yourself this late at night without a ride."

It wasn't my intention to be by myself, Pauline thought.

There was hardly time to strike up a conversation on the drive home. Warren Street was just up West Church Street and across East Railroad Avenue.

"Let your dad know I'm still praying for him. I'm not giving up until I get your whole family at church."

John Hutto's sincerity and hospitality might have been the one thing that would encourage Frank to go. Unfortunately, the fact that Elizabeth attended was Frank's primary reason for abstaining. Sunday mornings and evenings offered him his only tranquil moments at home.

"Thank you for the ride."

What could have happened? I hope he is alright. He would never not show up. She fought back tears as she walked up to her house.

Frank was packing his lunch box when Pauline entered the side door to the kitchen. "Hi, Rosebud. Aren't you home early? I thought you had a youth activity tonight." He spoke so seldom anymore; the sound of his voice was quietly reassuring.

"No, Daddy. Not tonight. I'm going to go up to bed. I'm feeling a little tired." She hurriedly kissed her father, accidentally transferring a tear onto his cheek. She then rushed up the stairs, not wanting her father to ask any more questions, not wanting to reveal her emotions. Frank gently wiped the moisture from his cheek. Rubbing the abandoned tear between his fingers, he got up from the table to follow her.

"Frank? Frank, was that Pauline?" Elizabeth yelled from the living room.

"Yes, Liz. She went up to bed. She said she was tired."

"Ha! Tired. What does she do to be tired? Frank, your daughter needs to be more responsible."

Frank shook his head and thought to himself, *well, she did come home...*

The tear was forgotten, replaced by the sound of Elizabeth's shrill voice. "You better keep an eye on her, Frank. She is going to get into trouble. You don't know who she is running around with. She never brings any of her friends home." Elizabeth filled her lungs. "And, clean up your mess when you finish in there. I have a hard enough time picking up after the kids. I don't need to be cleaning up after you."

Frank thought to himself in Italian, *For better or for worse, God? When will it get better?*

Pauline lay in her bed, tears streaming down her cheeks. The one person she could trust—and needed to be with tonight, left her alone. From her bed, between quiet sobs, she heard the downstairs telephone ring. She waited.

Frank picked up the handset, "Hello? Hello?" The only response was a hollow dial tone.

"Who is it?" Elizabeth barked from the living room.

"There was nobody there, Liz," Frank responded.

"That's happening all the time! Call the phone company tomorrow, and see if there is something wrong with the line," Liz ordered.

Pauline's tears were replaced with a smile; he was all right. Pauline pulled out her diary and wrote:

Where were you? What happened? My heart wanted so to be with you tonight. Thank you for letting me know you are all right. Tonight my heart will find contentment with you in my dreams. Good night, my love.

CHAPTER THIRTY-EIGHT
WHAT WAS THE RESPONSE?

"So, were Marc and Pauline able to keep their times together clandestine?" I asked as I took the last bite of my cheeseburger.

"For the most part, they were. Paige remained suspicious, but when the youth group was together, Pauline appeared to be spending more time with Jerry."

"Did Paige make any advances toward Marc?"

"Oh, she certainly did." He laughed. "Peggy told me the smell of fresh apple pie wafted throughout Monroe Township for months."

I joined him in the laughter.

"How did the youth group respond to Alonzo's leaving?"

"Actually, it went very well. Pastor Alonzo took counsel from his son and presented the selection committee with the comments and suggestions the youth group compiled. Peggy said the committee met with the youth group several times before making a final selection and calling Alonzo's replacement."

"How did Pauline respond?"

"Pauline wasn't there."

CHAPTER THIRTY-NINE
INTIMACY
DECEMBER 1959

She'd fought her feelings for so long, never intending anyone to be hurt.

She could never have imagined the chain of events leading to their intimacy. Fear mingled with fulfillment. She justified her feelings and condoned their secrecy.

In Pauline's mind, God is good—and for the first time in her life, Pauline felt good.

No one needed to know; it was no one's business. Their secret would never be exposed.

Just be careful.

CHAPTER FORTY
UNEXPECTED GUEST
MARCH 1960

"What's the matter with you? Eat your dinner."

"I'm not hungry, Momma."

"Ah, you're not hungry. I slave over a hot oven while you are out eating ice cream with your boyfriends, and you tell me you're not hungry. Eat your dinner! Frank, tell your daughter to eat her dinner."

"Pauline, your mother is right. It's a nice dinner; please eat something."

"Daddy, I can't eat. I'll get sick. Momma, I am sure it is wonderful, but I can't." Pauline pushed herself away from the table and rushed down the hall to the bathroom. A few minutes later, she reappeared. "I'm sorry. I don't know what's wrong with me, but I can't even smell the food. Momma, I know it is good, but the smell is making me sick."

"What do you mean the smell makes you sick? What is wrong with you, huh?" Elizabeth's face suddenly turned ashen as she realized.

"You're pregnant! You're pregnant, aren't you? Are you pregnant? Tell me; tell your father; tell him!" Elizabeth picked up Pauline's

plate and threw it into the sink, sending shards of glass and frag-
ments of food across the countertop.

"I knew this would happen. I told you, Frank. I told you this
would happen!"

Continuing her verbal condemnation she shouted, "Shame and
embarrassment are all you've ever brought to this family!"

Frank sat, grief-stricken. Shock and disappointment left him
motionless. He absorbed every verbal assault Elizabeth hurled. Her
pious rant was only beginning.

"I told you. I warned you!" She turned her contempt directly at
Pauline.

Involuntary sobs emanated from deep within Pauline's soul.

Pointing an accusing finger inches away from Pauline's face, Elizabeth shouted, "She's a tramp, a tramp, Franklin! Face it, your
daughter is a tramp! And I'll guarantee one thing you can be sure of.
She has no idea who the father is—no idea whatsoever!"

Pauline's and her father's eyes met. His sadness, his paralyzing
anguish, was more than Pauline could bear. "Daddy, say something.
Please, Daddy. Please say something! Daddy, it's not that way!
Daddy, I'll die if I lose you. Daddy, please!"

Tears welled in her father's eyes. His lips quivered as his heart
searched for words but could find none.

Elizabeth looked up at the ceiling with her arms outstretched
and she screamed, "Oh, dear God, look what she has done! Look
what she has done to me! How can I ever face anyone?"

Peggy quietly sat across from Pauline's table setting, unwilling to
make the slightest move. She knew her sister had made a terrible
mistake, but the implacable attack spewing from her mother's lips
terrified her. Her father's lack of response left Peggy with a hopelessness she'd never experienced.

"Get out of my sight! Get out of my sight, you tramp; out of my
house!"

Frank interrupted, "Elizabeth! Please!"

"Please—please? Please what? Please ignore the fact that your daughter is a tramp, whoring herself around our neighborhood."

Pauline's voice was hardly audible, "Daddy?"

Her father never looked up. He timidly rubbed the edge of the table, imperceptibly shaking his head in reticent disbelief.

"He has nothing to say to you. Get out of my sight!"

Pauline ran up the stairs and threw herself on her bed. Her emotions wrestled between crippling fear and overwhelmed anger.

"Why, God? Why? Why do you hate me? What have I done? This was not supposed to happen. You could have stopped it! Why God—why me? Why is it always me? I want to die, God. Can you do that for me? Is that what will make us both happy? Is that what will make everyone happy? WHERE ARE YOU, GOD?"

There was no response. Pauline knew there would be no response—there never was.

Except for the child within her, Pauline was alone.

A sleepless night segued into morning's light. Hopelessness clung to Pauline. There was no escaping it. A knock at the door startled her. It was a gentle knock followed by a soft voice.

"Pauline? Pauline, can I come in?" The apprehension in Peggy's voice momentarily removed Pauline's thoughts about herself.

"You can come in, Peg."

The door slowly opened. Fifteen-year-old Peggy Bianchi entered Pauline's room, holding her Teddy bear.

"Pauline? Are you okay?"

"No, Peg. No, I'm not." Pauline sat up in her bed. She tilted her head back, attempting to catch her tears before they dropped. She forced a smile through her tears. Her outstretched arms eased her sister's misgivings.

Peggy rushed into the room and into Pauline's arms.

"I'm scared, Peg. I'm really, really scared!" Pauline cried as she stared at the ceiling.

"I'm scared too, Pauline. I don't feel good. My stomach hurt all night."

Pauline softly stroked her sister's head.

"What's going to happen, Pauline?"

"I don't know, Peg. I don't know. Daddy just sat there—he just sat there! He hates me too, just like Momma hates me."

"He doesn't hate you, Pauline." Peggy's innocence calmed Pauline.

Pauline's foreboding premonitions were unclear. She could sense her life would never be the same.

"I'm in a lot of trouble, Peggy. I don't know what is going to happen, but I want you to know I love you."

Elizabeth called from the kitchen, "Girls, come down here. Breakfast is on the table."

"Oh, no!" Peggy whispered.

"It's all right, Peggy. You go downstairs. I'll be there in just a sec." Peggy was reluctant to leave Pauline. "Go ahead, Peg; I promise. I'll be right down. I just want to freshen up first."

Peggy reluctantly left the room.

Pauline made her way into the bathroom. She hoped the cold water would reduce the swelling around her eyes. She would not allow her tears to be the source of her mother's amusement.

"Pauline? Pauline, dear. Are you coming down? I don't want your eggs to get cold."

The passive lilt in her mother's voice served only to increase Pauline's dread.

Pauline entered the kitchen and sat at the table.

"Good morning, dear. Did you have a nice sleep?"

Pauline kept her head down. "I slept fine, Momma."

Elizabeth's smirk oozed through oleaginous words—slapping Pauline with hypocrisy. "I'm so glad you slept well. You'll need a good breakfast, sweetheart. I've packed you and your father a nice lunch. You've got a long trip ahead of you."

"What do you mean, 'long trip?' Where am I going?"

Elizabeth dropped her cloak of deceit, but she continued with her syrupy tone of voice. "Well, sweetheart. You are going out of my sight, out of my house, out of my life, until you decide to become a responsible member of this family."

Pauline was struck with panic. "Momma, what are you saying?"

Pauline's father entered from the garage. "Franklin, tell your daughter what we've decided."

Pauline's father was visibly shaken. "Pauline, your mother thinks—"

"Franklin!"

"Your mother and I think it would be better if you stay with Aunt Lilly for a while. At least until... until the baby is born."

Elizabeth interrupted, "We've decided to find an appropriate adoption agency so the child is raised by responsible parents."

Elizabeth positioned herself directly behind Pauline. Her mocking continued as she fondled a few strands of Pauline's hair. "Who knows? Perhaps even you will grow up while you're away."

Elizabeth paused and asked Pauline, "How are your eggs, dear?"

Pauline could not speak. She could not move. Even though she'd expected the worst, she was unable to fully comprehend the level of hatred her mother possessed.

Pauline was now in survival mode. There were no tears; there would be no argument. She was emotionally numb.

"Come now. We mustn't dawdle. Eat your breakfast and be gone."

Peggy began to hysterically scream, "No Momma, NO!"

"Peggy Lynn, you set yourself down and be quiet! You bring shame to this family and the same will happen to you! Let this be a lesson, young lady!"

Pauline quietly got up from the table. She walked over to her sister. While giving her a hug she whispered, "I will find a way to contact you. I promise I will find a way."

"Enough of this! Pauline, it is time for you to leave—it's long past time," Elizabeth chastised.

Pauline slowly looked up, directly into her mother's eyes. It was a look of total abhorrence. It was a vengeful, threatening look. So altered had Pauline's visage become so sinister her glare, Elizabeth took a step back.

A disquieting smile emanated from Pauline's lips. There was no emotion expressed—none whatsoever. A cold impression of finality adorned Pauline's response.

"You have never been more correct, Elizabeth Bianchi—long past time!"

Her father interrupted, "Pauline, that is your mother!" But Pauline's eyes never wavered from her mother's eyes.

"I have no mother! Daddy, get me out of here!"

CHAPTER FORTY-ONE
AUNT LILLY
1960

The drive from Monroe Township to New London, New Hampshire, took just under eight hours. Lillian Greco, Aunt Lilly, eagerly awaited her niece's arrival. She tempered her anticipation; she was fully aware this was not a time for celebration but a time for restoration. Aunt Lilly hoped to offer Pauline far more than a place to stay.

Lilly was the antithesis of her younger sister, Elizabeth. She was selfless and sincere—others oriented. Lilly was slow to judge, quick to praise, and always willing to open her heart and home to anyone in need.

From her front porch, she watched Frank's car turn onto her long driveway from the highway. A cloud of dust followed the approaching automobile. She nervously replaced the errant strands of hair behind her ear and wiped her hands on her apron as the car pulled into the driveway. Aunt Lilly greeted Pauline with a broad and loving smile.

Pauline and Frank waited for a moment, allowing the dust surrounding the car to fall to the ground. Pauline was the first to open the door. Aunt Lilly's hug was appropriately sincere, warmly offered, and gently applied. Pauline could not conceal her emotions.

"Oh, Aunt Lilly. I'm so scared!" Pauline cried into Lilly's shoulder.

"Come now, beautiful. We're not scared. We can do anything together!"

"You won't leave me; you won't throw me out. Will you?"

"Throw you out? Why, sweetheart," she gently laughed, "I haven't even let you in yet!" She kissed Pauline on the forehead as she smiled across the windshield at Frank who was just then exiting the car.

"Hello, Frank. I'm guessing you could use a hot cup of freshly brewed coffee."

"Lilly." Frank took a deep breath, "I'd like that. I'd like that a lot."

Lilly put her arm around Pauline and walked her toward the porch. Frank followed. She opened the screen door and moved Pauline across the threshold. Pauline was left standing just inside the living room. Her aunt and father were just outside. There was an awkward moment as Pauline stood looking back at her aunt and father still standing on the porch.

"Are you two coming in?" Pauline asked.

"We're coming in, dear. I want you to have a moment to realize you are at home. No one is ever going to throw you out." Lilly stepped into the room and hugged Pauline. "This is your home for as long as you wish."

Frank stood awkwardly outside. He held a paper bag as the screen door closed behind Lilly.

"Frank, come in here. Your daughter needs you, and you need her. And I need to get you that cup of coffee."

As Frank opened the screen door and stepped into the room, Pauline ran to his arms. His hug was, at first, hesitant. Hers was a desperate hug—a hug as if her father was her only lifeline. His tightening embrace assuaged her fear of his rejection.

"I love you, Rosebud. You will always be my princess; my fair maiden."

"Daddy, why do we have to do this? Why?"

"Your mother thought it would be better; better for you."

"Your wife thought it would be better for her!" Pauline responded.

"Pauline, that's no way to refer to your mother," Frank said in a patient and understanding tone.

"I am no longer referring to her as my mother. I no longer will—never, Daddy. Never!"

There was a moment of silence. The three realized the situation was irreversible. There were no appropriate consoling words, no way of drawing their arrival to a comforting conclusion.

"Lil, I probably should get going."

"That's nonsense, Frank. You just got here. You have to give yourself some time to rest before making that drive back." Lilly advised.

"No, no, that's okay. I'll be all right."

"Rosebud, I brought something for you. Peggy wants you to take care of him for her." Frank opened the paper bag he'd brought in. He removed the throw covering the tattered stuffed animal Peggy had asked him to deliver to Pauline.

"Teddy! Oh, thank you, Daddy. Thank you!" Pauline once again clung to her father's arms. "Don't go yet. Please don't go!" Pauline begged.

"Rosebud, I have to; I have to. I will see you soon." He paused, choking back poorly contained emotions. "I'll call every day. You'll see. This will all be behind us very soon. Right now, it is best—it is best for everyone. I love you." Frank peeled himself away from Pauline's grasp.

His car slowly drove away, down the long unpaved driveway. He looked to the right and the left before turning onto the highway. The dust behind his car settled. One final glance in the rearview mirror stamped the image of Pauline holding her sister's tattered Teddy bear on his broken heart.

CHAPTER FORTY-TWO

I NEVER KNEW...

I sat in the booth at St. Elmo, stunned. Responding to this new revelation I said, "I never knew Pauline had a child."

"No one did—well, no one outside of the family knew for sure. Elizabeth obscured Pauline's disappearance as an urgent move to care for her ailing aunt."

"Wasn't anyone suspicious? I asked.

"Of course, they were; most probably suspected the truth. No one would speak of it. It was more comfortable to ignore reality and accept Elizabeth's explanation."

"What about the youth group?"

"They had their suspicions, I'm sure. Paige and Marc called Mrs. Bianchi from time to time, inquiring how Pauline was, how her aunt was, and when Pauline might be returning home. Elizabeth politely took their calls. She would feign a broken heart and lament Pauline's newfound love for New Hampshire."

"It wasn't what we'd intended," she told those who inquired. "We do so miss our daughter."

He paused. "Peggy knew better than to speak otherwise. And

Frank... Frank slipped further and further into a deepening depression. They say a broken heart caused his rapidly declining health."

"Did Pauline tell her sister about the delivery? I mean, there's so much more to this story than I'd imagined."

"Peggy and Pauline communicated as much as circumstances allowed. Both were cautious. For a while, Peggy said she called Pauline from the telephone booth at Bray's to another telephone booth in New London. Peggy would call collect; Pauline would accept the charges. They would talk, set up a time for their next call, end their conversation, and simply walk away. There was no one left to charge for the call." He laughed. "Peggy said it lasted for only a brief period before the telephone company finally caught on."

"So, how did the pregnancy go? I mean, I'm guessing the baby was born healthy, right?"

CHAPTER FORTY-THREE
SECOND THOUGHTS
SEPTEMBER 1960

"Sweetheart, calm down. Everything is progressing as expected." Doctor Becker redirected his attention to Nurse Wilkerson. "Nurse, fifty milligrams of Meperidine." Turning back to Pauline, Doctor Becker said, "I'm going to give you something to calm you down and make you more comfortable." He gently patted Pauline's arm and wiped her forehead. "You and the baby are going to be fine, sweetheart. Just try to relax."

Pauline could feel the beads of perspiration soaking her scalp. Tears flowed from her eyes. She wondered if she had made the right decision.

Nurse Wilkerson, a young woman perhaps in her midthirties, reentered the room with the medication. She set the tray on the cart at the foot of Pauline's bed and filled the syringe for Doctor Becker. "Here you are. Fifty milligrams, doctor."

"That's correct," he said, turning his attention back to Pauline. "Fifty milligrams will do the trick." Doctor Becker took the syringe from Nurse Wilkerson. She stepped forward toward the left side of Pauline's bed and applied a cool compress to Pauline's forehead as Doctor Becker administered the injection. Pauline felt a warm sensation flowing through her body as the Meperidine made its way through her veins. She took a deep breath, a breath of relief.

"There now. Don't you feel better?" Nurse Wilkerson asked. Pauline nodded.

"Pauline, you are coming along very nicely. We've got you and the baby monitored and will be watching closely from the front desk. Try to get a little rest. We're going to have some work to do in the next few hours."

Doctor Becker and Nurse Wilkerson left the room.

Pauline had never felt more alone.

Questions raced through her soul—too many questions to even consider resting. Was her baby a boy or a girl? Would the baby be healthy? Would she get to see her baby, hold her baby—just once—just for a moment? Would the adopting family be good to her child? What will the baby's first steps be like? Whom will the baby resemble? How could she be so close to her child and yet so far away? What had she done? What had she given up? Did she make the wrong decision? Was it ever really her decision? In a matter of hours, she would be stripped of the one person closest to her, the one person she would forever hold dear to her heart. She would be condemned to quietly celebrate every birthday of her child alone. She would imagine her child's school years, graduation, and marriage. It was too late. In giving away her baby, Pauline now realized she'd given herself away.

The medication was indifferent to Pauline's emotional pain. The room spun as a swirling took over Pauline's consciousness, and she lightly dozed into a momentary sleep.

Doctor Becker approached the adoptive parents who were seated in the waiting room area. "She is doing very well. We have a monitor on the baby, and everything is progressing normally."

"Do you have any guess as to how long before our baby is born?" the gentleman asked.

"Well, sometimes these things take a while. The birth mother is young. If it goes too long, we will induce, but right now, my guess is another three to five hours." Doctor Becker replied.

The gentleman hugged his wife. She too was overcome with questions and emotions. Would her baby grow to love her as his or her mother? Would her baby grow to understand the love she and her husband have had from the very beginning? Will their baby ever feel rejected? What about the birth mother? Who is she? What brought her to this night—this moment? Was she a troubled girl? Was she a good girl who'd simply made a mistake? Would she remember her child? What would cause any woman, even a young girl, to give up this moment of joy? Is it a love too big to comprehend or an irresponsibility too easily forgotten?

"Thank you, doctor. Please make certain she is comfortable," the woman said, trying to connect words that would convey her heart. "And please let her know her child will always be loved and cared for. Let her know she can be proud of who her child will become."

Doctor Becker tilted his head forward, looking over his glasses. "I will make certain to convey your thoughts to her."

At 4:48 a.m. Pauline had been in her thirty-sixth hour of labor; it was a mournful labor, a labor that taxed Pauline's soul. The pangs of birthing were insignificant in comparison to the agony of a life being severed from the living. For thirty-six hours, Pauline suffered alone the unimaginable emotional consequences of her moment of gratification, her moment to be someone needed by someone else. Where was he now when she so desperately needed him? Where was he when their child was about to forever become a memory?

"Sweetheart, it's time," Doctor Becker's voice broke Pauline's painful imaginings. "Nurse, I want you to hold Pauline's hand. Pauline, I want you to do your best to relax between these last contractions."

Pauline didn't hear a word Doctor Becker said. She heard only the muffled sounds of oxygen escaping from the sides of the mask that hugged her face. It chilled the tears streaming down the sides of her cheeks. The pain in her heart swelled as her body involuntarily released the only one who might have ever brought her joy. Thirty-six hours passed far too quickly. *Oh, for a few moments more,* Pauline quietly begged. She struggled to catch a glimpse of her child, just a glimpse. Tears obscured her vision. She saw only the blurred image of Doctor Becker's green scrubs as he exited the delivery room with her child.

"You did well, sweetheart," Nurse Wilkerson said as she wiped Pauline's face. "You were perfect."

"My baby! How is, how is my baby?" Pauline sobbed.

"Your baby is beautiful, beautiful and healthy, sweetheart. We're going to help you sleep right now. The doctor will be back to finish and we will clean you up and take you to your room," consoled the nurse.

An orderly entered the delivery room to assist Nurse Wilkerson. As he entered, the swinging door momentarily ushered in a distant conversation between the adoptive parents and Doctor Becker.

"A boy, honey. We have a baby boy!"

The door swung closed—the voices, lost—gone forever with a part of Pauline she would struggle to forget—and forever remember.

She awoke in a sterile room, alone.

CHAPTER FORTY-FOUR
LEAVING THE HOSPITAL
1960

Exuberant families celebrated as they huddled around the nursery windows to catch glimpses of their newest arrivals. Pauline, her recovery room just down the hall, sank deeper into depression.

Doctor Becker moved her from recovery into a private room on the second floor. Still, the image of the delivery room door swinging shut, the sounds of joyful celebrations, and the smell of talcum powder would forever be seared into Pauline's memory.

She was released to her Aunt Lilly's care eight days after having given birth to a child she would never know. Aunt Lilly did her best, in the most difficult of circumstances, to offer Pauline a welcoming home without evading the reality of Pauline's loss. Love was all Aunt Lilly had to offer. It was a love Pauline only imagined existed.

"Pauline, you've been through a great deal, more than anyone your age should have to endure."

"It was all my fault, Aunt Lilly." Pauline wrapped herself in her despair.

"Fault is not something we will focus upon in this house. Guilt and blame are not the stepping stones to restitution, my dear. Life is messy. Don't kid yourself. It is messy for everyone." She lovingly stroked Pauline's hair. "Pauline, this—this event, this moment in your life is hard; hurtful. I am here with you. God is here with you."

Pauline shuddered. "God?"

"Pauline, don't let your loss and pain keep you away from the One who knows you best and loves you most."

Pauline interrupted, "Where was God when I needed Him? Why did He let this happen? Sure, He was with me—watching."

"Pauline!"

"No, Aunt Lilly. God could have stepped in! He could have stopped this from happening! He could have—"

Aunt Lilly lovingly hugged Pauline as she gently interrupted Pauline's ascending rant.

"He could have stopped your pregnancy instead of keeping you and your baby safe. He could have turned His back on you, your baby, and the family who, no doubt, had been praying for a child they could not bear. He could have done so many things that would have hurt so many people. Instead, He was quietly there, protecting, loving. Pauline, He remains here still loving unconditionally, still protecting without judgment."

Lilly's thoughts seemed to flash back to her own experiences in life. She continued stroking Pauline's hair. "I don't expect you to understand or even accept any of this right now. God has graciously given you to me, and I promise to love you and care for you. We will make it together."

"Thank you for not hating me. I love you, Aunt Lilly."

"Hate you? Silly girl. I've prayed for you your entire life! I never raised a child. Before you were even born, when your mother called with news of her pregnancy, I prayed for you. I loved you then; I love you now. Young lady, I am proud of you." She once again hugged Pauline. This time Pauline could sense a difference. This time it was a hug that, for some reason, felt God-like. "Pauline, I am so grateful to have you with me."

"Aunt Lilly, I am so angry. Angry with God, angry with Daddy, angry with the church, and my so-called friends. I am so angry I want to scream!"

Lilly did not say a word. She patiently, lovingly waited for Pauline to purge her innermost feelings—knowing if she did not, those feelings might cripple Pauline's soul.

"I am angry with them all, Aunt Lilly—BUT I ABSOLUTELY HATE MY MOTHER!"

"Pauline..." Aunt Lilly tried to interrupt, to assuage such talk of hatred.

"I know what I feel, Aunt Lilly. I hate her!" Pauline pushed herself up from the sofa where she had been sitting with her aunt. "She never loved me. I was a mistake, a curse. To her, I was as disposable as my baby. AND IT WAS MY BABY! My baby wasn't hers to give away. That was wrong, Aunt Lilly! That was wrong!"

Pauline paced, screaming through tightly clenched teeth, arms flailing at the open space around her.

"I HATE HER! I WISH SHE WAS DEAD!"

Pauline's sudden transformation stunned Aunt Lilly. "Pauline! I will not allow that kind of talk in my house!"

"What kind of talk, Aunt Lilly? Truth? Does everyone run away from the truth when it makes them uncomfortable? Is the truth only appropriate when it makes everyone around you feel good? When it makes you cringe, does it make it any less truthful? I hate my mother. I am certain I wasn't born hating my mother, she worked for it. It's the only thing she ever actually earned; and she earned it, Aunt Lilly. She earned it."

Pauline shrugged her shoulders with mock laughter. "I'm offended I have any feeling for her at all—even hatred!"

What began as a purging of emotions had evolved into a horrifyingly dark expression of abhorrence.

"If my hatred for that woman means I have to leave, I'll leave. If the talk of my hatred is not allowed, I will respect your wishes and be silent, but it doesn't change the truth."

"We'll not talk of her, Pauline. Right now, I want you to feel at home—your home. We'll not talk of her again."

Aunt Lilly invitingly patted the cushion where Pauline had previously been seated. Pauline returned and placed her head on her aunt's lap. Lilly once again stroked Pauline's hair.

"Aunt Lilly?" Pauline asked.

"Yes, dear?"

"I don't know who I am or who I was supposed to be. It isn't fair. It isn't fair at all."

CHAPTER FORTY-FIVE

LOSS AFTER LOSS...

The irony was too much for me to immediately grasp. The ice in my glass had melted, and I wondered if my heart was similar. His story, her pain. It was incomprehensible. I'd all but forgotten we were talking about the woman I'd known as Pauline Haughton—*Old Sweet & Sour*.

"How long did Pauline stay with her Aunt Lilly?" I asked.

"New London, New Hampshire became Pauline's home. Aunt Lilly became the only mother Pauline had ever known. It was unconditional love that Lilly offered. It was the only time Pauline felt safe immersing herself in another person's promise of love. For a brief time, a very brief time, Pauline was at peace," he answered.

"Why a brief time?" I asked.

"Lilly became ill. It started with a simple back pain. Lilly thought she'd pulled a muscle. It wasn't long, however, before the pain became more prominent in her lower abdomen. This was followed by rapid weight loss. Lilly was diagnosed with cancer. Pauline became the nurse, and Lilly the patient. Pauline stayed with her aunt throughout her illness until Lilly's passing in 1962."

"And then she returned home?" I assumed.

"Like I said, Pauline would never consider Jamesburg home. In Pauline's mind, everyone but Peggy had turned their backs on her. New London was her home. Aunt Lilly accepted Pauline as her own. There were no conditions, no boundaries."

"And that too was taken away from her."

"As was everything else that was meaningful to Pauline," he concluded.

"When news of Lilly's illness reached Elizabeth, she called daily. Lilly was not naïve. Lilly knew the reason for her sister's newfound interest in her well-being. Other than Pauline and Peggy, Elizabeth was Lilly's only living blood relative. She'd never married and had no children of her own. There was no immediate family member to leave her estate to, that is, *unless she left it to Elizabeth.*" He let that settle over the table for a moment while I gathered my thoughts.

I found myself lost in a myriad of unintended emotions. It wasn't guilt, not exactly. I found myself wrestling with my lack of understanding for Pauline. My thoughts were now riveted on this young woman, riddled with guilt, angry with God, yearning for companionship, alone without family, void of identity, left only with one instinctive emotion—anger!

He could see my consternation. I thought to myself, *stop this silly emotional response! Remember, this is Pauline we are talking about.*

"When did she become so hateful? I mean, I know it wasn't just me. No one liked her!" I reached for explanations.

"She didn't like herself," he responded. "I don't know if I can answer your question. I seldom witnessed the personality you wrote about."

"She was so cutting, so demeaning," I said as I struggled to make sense of the years I'd spent with her. "It's as if she wanted to be hated."

"It was about a year after Lilly's passing that Pauline's father became gravely ill."

"Of course he did!" I said, matter-of-factly. "Why not? Everyone else Pauline cared about was taken from her."

"Not quite everyone. Pauline still had her relationship with Peggy." He reminded me.

"If I were Peggy, I would have kept my distance. The mortality rate for people involved with Pauline was beginning to seem unusually high." I responded.

"As I was saying, Pauline's father became gravely ill. Pauline had a decision to make. Would she return to Jamesburg, or would she turn her back on her father the way she felt he'd turned his back on her?"

"Well? What did she decide?"

CHAPTER FORTY-SIX
THE RETURN
AUGUST 1963

Elizabeth was not at home. Peggy knew it was the perfect time to contact Pauline. She took her mother's directory from the kitchen drawer; Lillian Greco, Jefferson 7-6993. The telephone rang. Pauline answered.

"Hello?" Pauline's voice had an edge to it that Peggy was becoming accustomed to.

"Hi, Pauline. It's Peggy."

"Peg. Oh, my gosh! Sis, it's so good to hear your voice. How are you?"

"I can't talk long," Peggy responded. "I'm surviving this place—barely. I wanted to call and let you know Daddy is very sick. Pauline, the doctors say he may not survive the summer. I think, I think you should come home."

"Peggy, how did this happen? What's wrong with him? Why wasn't I called earlier?"

Pauline stopped her questioning. She knew why she wasn't informed of her father's illness. She was no longer considered part of the family. Pauline was now torn between the latent love of her father and the visceral hate she possessed for her mother. However, this may be her last opportunity to see her father alive.

"Peggy, are you certain? Is Daddy that ill? I don't want to come; I do not want to be around that woman! I know you can't control her, but believe me, if she dares to approach me, I will not be responsible for what I say or do!"

"Pauline, please don't come looking for a fight. I want to see you. If Daddy dies without you seeing him one last time, you will never forgive yourself. I will be alone here. I need you. I need you here now."

"Peg, I will never leave you, but I cannot permanently return to Jamesburg. I will not put myself under the hypocritical scrutiny of my family, my friends, the church, and that community—never again!"

"Just come home until...," Peggy's throat grew thick with emotion, "until you have to go back."

"I'll leave New London in the morning and should be there by late afternoon, early evening," Pauline relinquished.

"I'll change the sheets on your bed, and you can stay in your room," Peggy said.

"No, Peggy. I will not stay in the same house with that woman. I'll get a room at the Motor Lodge. I'll only be using it for sleep and will be with you most of the time during the day."

"Okay, Pauline. I'll see you tomorrow." Peggy felt conflicted. Even though their father was ill, Peggy could not contain a feeling of excitement. She would be reunited with her sister.

Pauline hung up the telephone and made preparations for her return to Jamesburg. As she prepared her suitcase, she suddenly felt a surge of anxiety. Who would she see? What questions would they ask?

Why did she even care?

Pauline had a restless night. What little sleep she got was fraught with nightmarish visions of her mother ripping her baby from her arms and fleeing into the dark cold night. Pauline could not scream, and she couldn't move. She was paralyzed with fear and hopelessness. She awakened in a sweat—her heart racing. The sound of its pounding echoed in her head. She lay there struggling to sleep, fearful of the images her slumber might give rise to.

The next morning was a new day. Gone was the previous night's anxiety. A steadfast resolve replaced the dread Pauline had previously felt. It was inevitable. She knew she would, at some point, come face to face with her mother. Somehow, her hatred had wrought a dark anticipation of the event.

The trip was a trip of necessity. As the odometer chipped away at the miles between New London, New Hampshire and Jamesburg, New Jersey, Pauline's sense of frustration heightened, with it, her level of anger. Once again, life's circumstances forced her to do something against her wishes.

Elizabeth Bianchi would do well to avoid Pauline.

CHAPTER FORTY-SEVEN
PAULINE'S ARRIVAL
1963

Pauline drove down Buckelew Avenue and onto East Railroad Avenue. One more turn and she would reach her destination. Perhaps it was a bit of sentiment that caused Pauline to drive past Paige's home. Perhaps a sense of unfinished business drove her past First Reliance Baptist Church. Pauline mockingly laughed at the church marquee that said,

> *"There's No Place Like Home!*
> *The Prodigal Son Returns*
> *Pastor Alonzo Ricci Sr."*

Pauline's interest in the neighborhood faded away. It was time to see her father. She continued on West Church, crossing over West Railroad Avenue, and she turned left onto East Railroad Avenue. A right turn onto Warren Street and she was moments away from her destination.

Pauline parked the car aside the curb and walked up to the

door. Before she could knock, Peggy threw the door open, and without a word, she embraced her sister. Peggy sobbed as she held Pauline.

"Oh, Pauline. I have missed you so much," Peggy sobbed.

"Peggy, I have missed you too." Pauline held Peggy at arm's length to view the young lady she had so quickly become.

"My goodness, girl! You're all grown up! Has that much time passed?" Pauline commented.

"Too much time, big sister. Come on in. Mother is not home. I told her you were coming. Let's just say, I might have to move up with you!"

"You mean she wasn't thrilled by word of my return? I'm shocked," Pauline mocked. The two girls giggled.

"Let me take your coat, Pauline. What do you have in the bag?" Peggy asked.

"It's a dear friend of mine. I've often held him close, but he was very eager to return." Pauline handed Peggy the bag.

"TEDDY!" Peggy gasped. "Pauline, you didn't have to do that. I gave him to you."

"And he did everything you wanted him to do. He made me feel comfortable and loved. Most importantly, when I held him at night, I would think about you and how much I wanted to one day thank you for him and for never giving up on me."

Peggy hugged the tattered bear.

"I think you could use him now, Peg. He's a very good listener."

"Pauline, let's go up and see Daddy. I think he is having a pretty good day today," Peggy said.

"Wait a minute, Peg. First, what is wrong with him? What do the doctors say? Is there any hope?" Pauline's eyes blinked back tears.

"It's his lungs. The smoking finally took its toll. You remember how he smoked before you left. Afterward, I don't think I ever saw him without a cigarette. It is really terrible. On bad days, he struggles to take a breath."

"Let's go up," Pauline said.

"Daddy, I have a visitor for you," Peggy sang as she reached the top of the stairs.

Pauline entered the bedroom. Frank immediately sprang from the bed and wrapped Pauline in his arms. "If you aren't the prettiest thing these old eyes have seen in years!"

"Daddy, Daddy, be careful! Get back in bed," Pauline demanded while intensely embracing him.

"Nonsense, Rosebud. I have never felt better. Girls, give me this moment. I don't know how many more I'm gonna have like it, and I want to enjoy it completely," Frank replied.

Peggy joined the hug in Frank's arms. The three embraced. Tears streamed from everyone's eyes. Each one talked over the other, sharing their love, their memories, and hugging more intensely with each story.

No one heard the front door open or the steps coming up the stairs. Frank's grip loosened when he looked at the doorway.

"What is going on here? Frank, get back in that bed!" Elizabeth shouted.

Pauline slowly turned. Her eyes blazed with hatred. Her face contorted as her jaws clenched. Elizabeth stood motionless. Her lips appeared to attempt to form words, but nothing came out.

To the shock of everyone in the room, Pauline slowly and deliberately said in Italian, "*Vai fuori di qui! Questo è il mio momento e non te ne prendi un attimo di più. Hai preso tutto ciò che mi è caro. Non questa volta!*" (Get out of here! This is my moment, and you don't take a second longer. You took everything dear to me. Not this time.)

Elizabeth recoiled from the doorway. Pauline's voice matched the intensity and tone of Elizabeth's venom that she had spewed over the years. The sound of it sent Elizabeth backward against the railing. She screamed as she ran down the stairs and out the front door. The three could hear the car's tires screech as she sped away from the house. For the time being, there would be peace.

Frank slowly backed up to the side of the bed. Pauline and Peggy assisted him as he lay his head on the pillow. The silence was deafening. Finally, Frank was able to speak. "Rosebud, I must compliment you on your mastery of the Italian language." He struggled to take a deep breath. "I could not have said it better myself!" Frank closed his eyes while chuckling. The girls sat on either side of the bed and held his hands.

He squeezed their hands in contentment, chuckled, and repeated himself, "Bravo! Bravo, Rosebud. Very nicely done!"

CHAPTER FORTY-EIGHT
CARLOTTA WILLIAMS
1963

At five o'clock, Carlotta Williams knocked on the door and then let herself into the living room. Carlotta was Frank's home nurse. She visited Frank in the morning and in the evening to review his medications and keep a record of his vital signs.

"Hello, all y'all," Carlotta called out in her usual friendly tone.

Pauline entered the living room from the kitchen. "Excuse me. Who are you and why did you just let yourself into this house?"

"Well, sweetheart, I might just ask you the same thing, seeing as I am here twice a day to care for Mr. Bianchi and I've never met the likes of you."

Pauline introduced herself. "My name is Pauline. Mr. Bianchi is my father."

"Uh-huh, of course he is." Carlotta made certain her doubt was exaggerated. "And that's why I've never heard of you before. That's why there are no pictures of you anywhere." She looked directly through Pauline. Her stare was intimidating. "Who are you, really?"

"What do you mean? Who am I, really? I've told you who I am. I am Mr. Bianchi's eldest daughter. The fact that you've never heard of me is not surprising."

Peggy rushed down the stairs and hugged Carlotta. "Hi, Carlotta. I see you've met Pauline, my sister."

"Oh, so that's who this is. We were just getting to know one another," Carlotta said as she continued staring at Pauline over Peggy's shoulder.

"Pauline, this is Carlotta. She visits Daddy every—"

Pauline interrupted, "Yes, so she has told me, every day, morning and evening." Pauline turned her attention to Carlotta who had not taken her eyes off Pauline. "You'll have to forgive me for being startled when I came from the kitchen. I didn't expect—"

"A black woman standing in the living room?"

"I don't care what color you are. The fact you simply walked into this house startled me," Pauline tersely replied.

Carlotta knew differently. Once again, she hugged Peggy; once again, her eyes were fixed upon Pauline. In her best stereotypical black dialect, she said, "Miss Peggy. Y'all gonna have to excuse me. I has to check on the massa—see he been doin what the docta done told him to doos." Carlotta walked past Pauline and smiled as she made her way up the stairs.

"Carlotta has been a real help since Daddy got sick. She makes him laugh."

"Yeah, she's a real hoot," Pauline sarcastically replied. "Why a black woman? Didn't they have enough money to afford a—," Pauline suddenly realized she was unintentionally revealing hidden feelings, a secret prejudice. "What I mean is, couldn't they afford a professional?"

"Carlotta is a professional, Pauline. She is a very caring professional. Daddy looks forward to her visits; so do I."

The front door once again opened, and a sudden cold draft entered the room. Elizabeth had returned. Pauline immediately made her way up the stairs to say goodbye to her father. Confronting

Carlotta was far less daunting than once again confronting Elizabeth.

"Excuse me. Daddy, I have to get going, but I will be back first thing in the morning."

"Rosebud, having my two daughters here is the best medicine for me. Thank you. Thank you, from the bottom of my heart. You will never know how much this means to me. I love you."

"I love you, Daddy." Turning her attention to Carlotta, she said, "Carlotta, I am sorry for my actions downstairs. Thank you for taking care of my dad."

"Sweetheart, it's a pleasure to meet you. I promise he is in good hands," Carlotta politely responded.

Pauline turned and walked down the stairs. Peggy met her at the bottom of the stairs as her mother quickly passed into the kitchen.

"I love you, Pauline. Thank you for coming home. See you in the morning."

"In the morning, Peg," Pauline answered without taking her eyes off her mother's back.

As Pauline closed the front door behind her, she heard the all too familiar rage expel from her mother toward Peggy. She resisted the urge to return and defend her sister. Peggy would have to learn to defend herself.

At nine o'clock the next morning, Pauline returned. Peggy answered the door.

"Pauline, you have a key. Why don't you use it?" Peggy asked.

"This is not my home, Peggy. I'm just a visitor here, and I do not want to be mistaken for anyone else."

"Okay, but it seems kinda weird if you ask me," Peggy responded.

"I didn't hear anyone ask," Pauline sharply replied, and she made her way to the stairs. Peggy followed.

"Daddy slept well last night. I think it was because you are home

—I mean, here," Peggy said, and then she released a long, low sigh. She stumbled on the first step as she followed Pauline.

"Thank you, Peggy. Look, I didn't mean to be short with you. Being back here is hell for me. I don't mean being with you and Daddy. It's that woman. I feel her lurking, ready to attack if she senses my guard weakening. I hate her, Peggy. You might as well know it."

"So that's supposed to be breaking news? I know you hate her; everyone knows you hate her. She knows you hate her." Peggy grasped the banister for support.

"She may know I hate her—but she has no idea the level of hate. She just better stay completely away from me," Pauline whispered before entering their father's bedroom.

"Will you look at that, Carlotta! The good Lord is delivering more of that miracle medicine for me," Frank said as Pauline and Peggy stood in the doorway of the bedroom.

"Good morning, Pauline," Carlotta greeted.

"Good morning, Carlotta. How is our patient this morning?" Pauline asked with a practiced sticky sweetness.

"Well, I'd say he's fairing pretty well this morning. He seems to be quite excited about a couple of young ladies visiting him today," Carlotta responded as she moved the food tray from Frank's bed.

Frank sat up, and with outstretched arms, he invited his daughters into the room. "Get over here, you two. I want a double..." he struggled to catch his breath, "a double dose of loving this morning." His invitation was followed by convulsive coughing. Carlotta quickly returned to his side. She slipped something under his tongue.

"When you calm down, young man, I'll give you a sip of water." Carlotta turned to Pauline and Peggy. Hoping to calm their concerns, she said, "Would you look at that? Two pretty young things come to visit, and they take his breath away." She turned her attention back to Frank. Tenderly wiping his forehead, she said, "You better just behave yourself, else I'm going to have to get tough on you."

Frank chuckled, "Oh, Carlotta, I'm fine. I'm fine. Give me that sip of water so I can kiss my girls."

Carlotta smiled, handed Frank his water, and winked at Pauline and Peggy, urging them to enjoy the hug their father was offering.

Carlotta gathered a few things, set them on the tray, and excused herself. Pauline stiffened as she heard Elizabeth's voice confront Carlotta in the hallway.

Frank sensed Pauline's tension. Still hugging his daughters, he whispered in Pauline's ear, "Princess, there will be other days to slay the dragon. This is our moment."

The three shared precious time together. There was no thought given to the seriousness of their father's illness, no discussion of Pauline's leaving home. Laughter, long departed, filled the upstairs. Memories, only known by the heart—thought to have been forgotten, were resurrected.

By eleven o'clock, it became obvious Frank was tired. Peggy recognized his fatigue.

"Daddy, Pauline, and I are going to let you get some rest. We'll make a run to the store. Is there anything you need?"

"Sweetheart, I have everything I could ever want right here with me," he weakly stated.

The girls kissed their father on the forehead and exited the bedroom. Before reaching the bottom step, they could hear his familiar snore. They giggled. It was yet another memory to treasure.

CHAPTER FORTY-NINE
YOU'VE CHANGED
1963

Three years had passed since Pauline last drove the streets of Jamesburg. Not much had changed. As the girls drove past Bray's Pharmacy, memories erupted within Pauline at the sight of the telephone booth. Pauline thought to herself, *three rings, hang up, wait for the callback*. She chuckled.

"What are you thinking about, Pauline?" Peggy asked.

"Oh, I don't know. Just thinking," Pauline replied.

"Well, you must be thinking about something if you are thinking at all," Peggy said under her breath.

"I said I was just thinking!" Pauline retorted.

"Okay, okay. No need to bite my head off," Peggy replied.

"No need to keep asking."

"I won't."

Pauline slammed on the brakes. "ENOUGH! DO YOU HEAR ME? ENOUGH!"

Peggy's eyes instantly filled with tears. She'd underestimated the tension Pauline felt. Her verbal volley was just something sisters do, or so she thought. She didn't know if she should apologize or just sit quietly.

Pauline spoke first. "Look, I know you've been through a lot. I know Daddy's illness has only added to it. Sis, it can't be the same, it never will be the same. I've changed. I didn't ask for it. Change attacked me. It devoured my heart and soul and left me for dead." She turned her head and stared out the window.

Peggy sat motionless.

Pauline stoically continued, "I can't go back to who I was—ever. I don't even know that person. I only know she was someone I would never want to be again." Pauline placed her hand on Peggy's leg and looked her in the eyes. "Sis, I was weak; a pitiful human being. I had allowed myself to be abused, confused, and used. I had no identity, no place. I used to be alone in a crowd of people. Don't let that ever happen to you. You will soon be able to leave this wretched place. Stay strong. Don't let them change you. Don't let them rob you of who you are."

"I'm sorry, Pauline. I am so very sorry. I love you."

Suddenly, Pauline exuded an effervescence of excitement. She started driving down the road and pointing out sites and their sameness. The heaviness of the moment was abruptly broken. It was as if nothing previously had taken place. It was a frightening transition. A transition Peggy would never forget.

"Let's go to Bray's!" Pauline demanded.

"Let's what? Pauline, are you all right?" Peggy's mouth opened,

"Let's go to Bray's and celebrate!" Pauline repeated.

As she turned the car around, Peggy asked, "What are we celebrating?"

"Nothing!" Pauline giggled like a schoolgirl. "There is absolutely nothing to celebrate; ever. So, let's celebrate now!" Pauline shouted with exuberance.

She pulled into the parking lot and ran to the telephone booth. She dialed the number. Three rings. Pauline hung up and waited.

Nothing.

"Who were you calling? Peggy asked.

"No one!" Once again, Pauline laughed. She grabbed Peggy's hand and pulled her through the pharmacy doors.

"Hi, Mr. Bray!"

"Well, if it isn't... my word girl! Did you take a wrong turn somewhere?" Mr. Bray joked. "Where have you been?"

"That's exactly what I did, Mr. Bray. EXACTLY! I took a wrong turn—and we're celebrating a new destination." Pauline hysterically laughed and ran back to the soda fountain.

Mr. Bray looked to Peggy for answers. She rapidly blinked her eyes and shrugged her shoulders.

"Come on, Peg. Sit down," Pauline called from the rear of the pharmacy.

Peggy and Mr. Bray made their way to the soda fountain. Peggy sat next to Pauline, who was twirling around on her polished, chrome-based, red vinyl seat.

"How long you in town, kiddo?" Mr. Bray asked.

"Till my father dies, I suppose. I'll have a vanilla hot fudge sundae with Spanish peanuts and hot caramel sauce," Pauline responded without a hint of emotion.

Pauline's phlegmatic response took Mr. Bray by surprise. "I... I'm sorry to hear he has taken ill, Pauline. Dreadful sorry I am," Mr. Bray somberly replied.

"It happens. Now, would you mind getting my sundae?" A dismissive Pauline once again requested, punctuating her request with a haunting smile.

"Right away, dear. Right away." Turning to Peggy, Mr. Bray asked, "And for you, young lady?"

"I'll have the same, Mr. Bray. Thank you for your concern for our father." Peggy kept nervously shifting her eyes to Pauline.

Mr. Bray strode to the large containers of ice cream and began making the girls' sundaes.

"Pauline! What has gotten into you? You are acting like such a spaz!" Peggy scolded.

"Acting? Who's acting, Peggy? Everyone is fake. Nothing is real, nothing matters, everything is whatever you make of it—if you don't make something of it, someone else will." Pauline grabbed hold of the countertop and spun herself around. As the barstool made its third revolution and came to a stop, Pauline's demeanor once again was altered. Her piercing eyes looked through her younger sister. Slowly and in a hushed tone of voice, Pauline said, "You get what you can. You can what you get. You put a lid on the can, and you poison whatever is left! All that matters is that you survive."

Peggy shook her head in disbelief. "You don't really mean that."

"Don't I?" Pauline laughed once again. "Don't I, little sister?" Pauline's laughter resolved into an impetuous warning. "Don't be naïve, little one. Don't be naïve. Naivety is what they look for, what they prey upon. Heartlessness is what they fear!"

"Here are those sundaes and a couple of extra cups of hot fudge and caramel," Mr. Bray said proudly as he presented the sundaes to Pauline and Peggy. "Consider these on the house, ladies. Welcome back, Pauline."

Pauline stared at the sundae. "I wanted Spanish peanuts." Her eyes focused on Mr. Bray. "I asked for Spanish peanuts. Where are my Spanish peanuts?"

"Oh, my goodness, I forgot. Here, let me get you a couple of scoops of those nuts, and I'll fetch you an extra cup full." Mr. Bray apologized as he smiled and reached for Pauline's sundae.

"You'll have to make another sundae. The ice cream has begun to melt by now," Pauline scolded.

"I'm sure it's going to be fine—"

Pauline interrupted Mr. Bray, "You'll have to make another." She showed no emotion. She was firm, unimpressed by Mr. Bray's generosity, and unscathed by whatever he or her sister thought of her.

"Two more, in fact. My sister's ice cream has begun to melt also," Pauline concluded.

Peggy apologetically responded, "No, no, that's all right, Mr. Bray. Mine, mine is just fine—"

Pauline more forcefully interrupted, "Two!"

A shocked and puzzled Mr. Bray quietly responded, "Right away. Yes, two sundaes—right away, Pauline."

Turning back to Peggy, Pauline nonchalantly smiled. "Where do you want to go shopping?"

"Shopping? Shopping? Pauline, do you realize what you just did? How you spoke to Mr. Bray? Did you hear yourself?" Peggy's raised eyebrows sat high above her widened eyes that scanned the room, looking at potential observers of Pauline's bad behavior.

"I did."

"Don't you even care? Just a little?" Peggy almost whispered.

"No." Pauline boldly stated.

"What do you mean, 'NO?'" Peggy became more animated. "You were ungrateful; horrible!"

Again, Pauline spoke without emotion. "I will be grateful when I get my order the way I ordered it. I will be grateful when you stop preaching to me with your platitudes of how you believe I should respond. I will be grateful when I leave this wretched town." Pauline ran her fingers through her hair. "Where would you like to go shopping?"

Mr. Bray returned with two freshly prepared hot fudge sundaes, precisely as Pauline had ordered.

"Thank you so much, Mr. Bray. They look delicious! It's nice to see you again," Pauline gushed.

Mr. Bray glanced at Peggy, then once again at Pauline. "Uh, yes, yes. Uh, so very nice to see you again, Pauline. If you girls need anything else, I'll be at the front of the store." A confused Mr. Bray slowly left the girls to their sundaes.

They finished their hot fudge sundaes in silence and left the pharmacy. Before exiting Peggy turned to Mr. Bray, who was standing at the register. She waved, her lips forming the words, *I'm sorry*. Mr. Bray nodded his head in acknowledgment and smiled.

"Let's just go over to Gatzmer's and pick up a few things," Pauline suggested.

"Okay. Maybe we can buy a few things Momma doesn't allow Daddy to have and sneak them in to him," Peggy suggested.

"Now you're cooking with gas," Pauline said as she giggled with pleasure at the thought of defying any aspect of her mother's dictates.

At the stoplight, Peggy broke the silence. "Pauline?"

"Yes?"

"Was it hard?"

Pauline knew what Peggy was referring to. She could choose to avoid the question, attack Peggy for even broaching it, or take the risk of trusting her younger sister. Pauline chose to trust Peggy.

Pauline detoured to the park. There would be time to run by Gatzmer's later. She made Peggy promise to never divulge what she was about to say. Peggy promised. For the next several hours Pauline Bianchi told her sister everything. Peggy freely asked questions. Pauline just as freely answered them. Peggy would never feel the same way about her neighborhood, her church, and Pauline's former friends. Peggy's love for Pauline would never falter.

"They all left me, Sis. All of them. Some of them knew. Heck, who am I kidding? They probably all knew. But no one ever reached out to me."

He didn't even try.

CHAPTER FIFTY

PUT ON A FRESH POT!

"So, that's when Pauline bonded with Peggy and spilled the beans, so to speak," I said. St. Elmo was quiet. Only a few tables were occupied other than ours.

"That's when she began to bond. Over the years, Pauline's trust grew as her hidden vulnerabilities were openly displayed to her sister. As her confidences were never broken, her trust continued to grow. As years passed, Pauline's dependence on her sister's trust also grew."

"Might I get you more coffee, gentlemen?" Antonio asked.

"Antonio," I said, "I suggest you put on a fresh pot."

"Right away, sir."

"How long was Pauline in Jamesburg?" I redirected my attention to the storyteller.

"Their father quietly passed away three weeks after Pauline arrived. They were at home together when he passed. Their mother was at a ladies' luncheon. Peggy was going to call the church and advise her mother to return home. Pauline suggested their mother would not want to be interrupted." He gave me a mischievous smile.

"Were there further run-ins with her mother?" I asked.

"Pauline took every precaution to avoid her mother. Her contempt would benefit no one. If she were to expose her feelings in public, it would only serve to bolster her mother's lies and encourage pity for her from her friends. In Pauline's mind, her mother was dead. Pauline was satisfied with that."

"Did she see anyone in the old youth group, Paige, Trina?" I asked.

"Well, Peggy was dating Danny Miller, so she saw quite a bit of him, but they didn't talk. Some of the kids had already moved away. I just don't think Pauline cared to see any of them."

I hesitated to ask but had to know. "Did she see Jerry, or...," I was almost afraid to ask, "... or Marc?"

"Jerry was never mentioned. Marc? Well, Paige and Marc were an item, and although they knew Pauline was in town, neither of them made any effort to reach out to her."

"How did Pauline and my father-in-law meet? Did Peggy give you any insights?"

A smile broke across his face. "Oh, she told me more than just how they met. Your father-in-law had a powerful charm about him. He could be quite persuasive, in a disarming sort of way."

"What do you mean?" I asked.

"Pauline told Peggy he came across as very nonchalant when, in fact, he was quite calculating. His passive demeanor—almost naïve persona—precluded an individual's natural defenses. He always had an agenda. His objective was to encourage those whom he allowed into his world to comply with his agenda without them realizing he was controlling it. Before a person knew it, he was not only agreeing with Ben, but he was also acting as if it was his own idea."

"I've got to admit, you are spot on with your analysis," I said. "He was conniving but in a polite, sometimes playful sort of way. You knew you were being taken, but somehow you enjoyed the ride."

"It's funny you should use that analogy. Enjoying the ride was exactly how Ben and Pauline met."

"What do you mean?" I asked.

"It was a chance meeting, I suppose. Their two lives intertwined as a result of Pauline's endeavor to start life over, doing something she enjoyed doing. Sadly, there were few things Pauline experienced in her life that would be a catalyst to her future. However, there is one memory, one experience, Pauline recalled with pure enjoyment. Pauline loved to fly."

CHAPTER FIFTY-ONE

UP, UP AND AWAY

FEBRUARY 1970

P auline stepped off the elevator into a long corridor. The arrow pointing to the left read, "TRANS WORLD AIRLINES —202." There were numerous offices on both sides of the long corridor. Pauline adjusted her skirt, making certain it was at the proper length. Upon entering room 202, Pauline became the immediate center of attention. Eight young ladies, having already checked in, were seated and awaiting their interviews. The gauntlet of young women sized up Pauline as she walked past them toward the receptionist's desk.

"Hello. My name is Pauline Bianchi," she began. "I have a ten o'clock interview this morning."

"Good morning, Miss Bianchi," the receptionist graciously responded. "I am so happy you are here. I have a packet for you to review to help you prepare for your interview." The receptionist handed Pauline a large manila envelope. "Mr. Graham will be with you as soon as we call your name." She then indicated that Pauline sit next to the other girls already seated. "As you can see, this morning he has several interviews."

Pauline's heart sank. She was looking for anything that might give her a slight edge. With a nonchalant glance at the young woman's name badge, Pauline asked, "Miss Eberhart, might I ask you a question?"

"Certainly. What is it?" Lydia Eberhart folded her hands, giving Pauline her total attention.

"You have greeted me with such a wonderful smile and with such enthusiasm. Is that atmosphere created by Trans World Airlines, or do you simply bring that warmth to your job?"

Pauline noticed an involuntary smile come over the woman's face. "Miss Bianchi, that is such a wonderful thing for you to ask. I assure you, TWA is a wonderful family of employees who sincerely care for one another. Thank you for your wonderful compliment."

Pauline smiled. Turning back to the other applicants, she took one of the two remaining seats and opened the packet. She'd studied the corporation's requirements for hair, dress, and makeup and went to great lengths to duplicate that appearance for her initial meeting. It was obvious the other eight applicants had done the same.

Mr. Graham's door opened. A visibly distraught attractive young woman quickly exited the office and made her way to the elevator, past the seated women. She pushed the elevator button. She pushed it again; then again. Standing in front of nine seated women, her emotions were on display. She continued to frantically push the elevator button. Not willing to continue her humiliating performance for the snickering onlookers, she turned and ran to the stairs. Pauline was appalled by their responses. She felt the need to distance herself from their childish reactions. She stood, positioning herself a few feet away from them.

Much to Pauline's surprise, and the surprise of the other women, Miss Eberhart stepped forward and said with a smile, "Miss Bianchi, Mr. Graham will see you now." The seated ladies turned to one another, questioning how this latest candidate was called before any one of them.

Pauline casually glanced at the faces of the remaining seated young ladies. Offering only a polite smile, she once again endured the gauntlet of murmurings.

Miss Eberhart directed Pauline to the door the previous candidate had just exited. Pauline knocked on the door. "Oh, you can go right in, Miss Bianchi. Mr. Graham is expecting you." Pauline opened the door and found herself in a very large circular office. Situated directly across from her, Pauline estimated about thirty-five feet away, was a large mahogany desk. An impeccably dressed man with strikingly stern features sat at that desk. He appeared to be deeply entranced by the forms he reviewed.

Without looking up, the man announced, "Miss Bianchi?" His voice was forceful, so much so that it startled Pauline. Assessing the situation, Pauline realized her every movement from the door to the seat in front of the desk would be carefully scrutinized. She smiled and gracefully walked toward the desk.

"You can call me Pauline," Pauline offered.

"I will call you Miss Bianchi," the gentleman firmly responded as he studied Pauline's walk and turned his attention to her application, which Lydia Eberhart had given him. There appeared to be an additional note stapled to the application, a note Pauline had not submitted.

"As you wish," Pauline responded.

The gentleman quickly looked up from her application and sternly examined her over the edge of his glasses. Having the last word was a habit Pauline would have to curb.

"I DO wish, Miss Bianchi." There was no mistaking Mr. Graham's demonstration of his authority.

Pauline, although regretting her misstep, smiled confidently.

"Let's not waste any time," Mr. Graham dismissively stated. "You do realize representing Trans World Airlines is a full-time occupation. The requirements for such a position are often regarded as infringements upon the social lives of those who are fortunate enough to be employed by our organization."

Pauline smiled once again; he'd tipped his card. She knew from hearing the exploits and personal confessions from several stewardesses this life was by no means akin to the description Mr. Graham was expressing. She would be a stewardess, often flying to distant places, often experiencing layover times—layover times with attractive men who flew the planes. Seldom were flight crews found at Wednesday evening prayer meetings.

"Sir, I am well aware of the standards your company has set forth, and I already live by those standards in my personal life. Now is the perfect time for me to commit to working for such a well-respected company, and I would be very proud to represent TWA," Pauline responded without the slightest hesitation.

"A-hum." He went back to studying her application. "There has been a time you seem to have lived in New Hampshire. What were you doing there?"

Did he already know? Was this all a ruse, another means for life to humiliate her? Of course, she'd lied on the application. She could not say that she'd given birth and then given the baby away. Pauline did not immediately respond. She waited. She waited for him to look up from her application once again. It seemed like an uncomfortable length of time, but Pauline would not speak simply to fill dead air.

He looked up. "Did you understand my question?"

She responded, "I understood your question very well, sir, and was considering the best way to respond without playing upon your sympathy." Pauline's response gave her just a few moments more to fully formulate her explanation. "I've applied for this position because I have served all my life. I have set my own goals aside to care for the needs of others. My aunt lived alone in New Hampshire. When she became ill, it seemed to be too much of an inconvenience for others in our family to cater to her needs. I left Monroe Township to be at her side through her illness until she passed."

"I see. And what were your goals? The goals you say you gave up?"

"Sir, I am now attempting to fulfill them by working with your company. I hope to have a place where my services are appreciated, and I can grow with a group of individuals who share the same experiences." Thinking back to her communication with Lydia Eberhart she continued, "I have no close family ties to distract me from my commitment, and so my family would be Trans World Airlines."

Mr. Graham nodded his head in what Pauline considered to be an affirmation. "Have a seat, Miss Bianchi." Mr. Graham held his hand out to indicate a chair to the left of his mahogany desk. "Never been married? No children?" He asked as he read her written responses to those questions.

"No, sir."

"No boyfriend?" He asked.

Pauline shook her head, indicating she had no boyfriend; no personal attachments to anyone. As she did, a sense of loneliness swept over her. She realized how unintentionally truthful she was being.

"Well, why in tarnation not?" Mr. Graham responded with almost a shout. "Why in the world would a beautiful young lady like you not have a boyfriend? What's wrong with you that I don't know about?"

Pauline politely chuckled. "Mr. Graham, sir, I would be most grateful if you could help me find that out!"

Both Pauline and Mr. Graham laughed.

"Miss Bianchi, I like you. From the note attached to your application, it appears Miss Eberhart likes you too. She believes you would do very well with Trans World Airlines—I believe she is right! TWA will do very well having you on board. Mind you, it isn't easy. When we have non-stop flights, you have non-stop work. But I think you will be up to the challenge."

Pauline heard his words but struggled to believe they were coming from him. Mr. Graham was offering her the opportunity she dreamed of.

"Pauline, may I call you Pauline?"

Pauline paused. She tilted her head just slightly, pursed her lips firmly together, and squinted as if giving the request careful consideration. Mr. Graham recognized her playfulness and once again laughed.

"All right, all right! I will call you Miss Bianchi," he apologized.

"Pauline will be just fine, Mr. Graham, as long as I can call you my boss," Pauline laughed in response.

With that, Mr. Graham walked around the desk and thrust his hand forward. "Congratulations, Pauline. It is my pleasure to be the first to formally welcome you aboard Trans World Airlines!"

Pauline began to stretch her hand forward, but impulse replaced reason, and she gave Mr. Graham a bear hug. Fearing she'd once again betrayed herself with such recklessness, she immediately stepped back, adjusted her blouse and skirt, and apologized.

"Nonsense, young lady. I was counting on a hug!" Mr. Graham responded, setting Pauline's mind at ease.

She turned to exit only to find Lydia standing in the doorway. The excitement on Lydia's face added to the celebration already taking place in the room. She ran to Pauline and gave her a congratulatory hug.

"I knew it; I just knew it! I knew we would be working together. I am so happy. You are going to love TWA, and TWA is going to love you!"

Pauline reentered the corridor to find the chairs empty; the gauntlet was gone. As she looked down the empty corridor toward the elevator, Lydia walked up behind her.

"Pauline? Are you all right?"

Pauline chuckled, "Oh, yes, yes, Miss Eberhart. I am fine. I'm a bit in shock. What just happened?" She paused, then nervously continued, "Am I dreaming?"

Lydia responded, "No, Pauline. No, you are not dreaming! Welcome to our family. And since you are family, please call me Lydia." She took the envelope Pauline clutched and replaced it with a *Trans World Airlines—Employee Handbook.* "I do believe this is yours," Lydia said as she once again gave Pauline a welcoming hug.

CHAPTER FIFTY-TWO
WELCOME ABOARD
SEPTEMBER 1971

"Good morning. Welcome aboard Flight 37 with service from Philadelphia to Los Angeles, California. We'll be flying our Lockheed L-1011 TriStar at a cruising altitude of 38,000 feet. The weather in Los Angeles is going to be a bit warmer than our thirty-three degrees here in Philadelphia. The arrival temperature will be a balmy seventy-five degrees. Radar indicates a few heavy clouds ahead, so we might experience a few bumps. Please keep your seatbelts buckled for your comfort and safety as well as the safety of those around you. We've got a great meal planned during our flight and our beverage service will begin shortly after take-off. So, sit back, relax, and if there is anything your TWA team can do for you, we look forward to serving."

Pauline would be serving in the suite with crew mate Dorothy Skinner. The eighteen-sleeper suite was spacious, including three rows, six seats per row, separated by two aisles that provided two comfortable seats per section. They would be flying light today with only 103 passengers aboard the 272-seat TriStar.

Pauline looked over the passenger manifest. Twelve passengers were assigned to the suite. There were no special needs listed, and no unusual requests. Each passenger entering the suite was warmly greeted by Paul and Dot.

As he ducked his head entering the cabin, Mr. Haughton immediately caught Pauline's eye. She reached for his seat assignment and quickly crosschecked his name. "Welcome aboard, Mr. Haughton. My name is Pauline. I'll be happy to serve you today. Can I get you a special beverage before take-off?"

"Hi, Pauline. So, you will be taking care of me today, huh? Super, Super."

Pauline noted a charming glint in the gentleman's eye and perceived a vailed flirtation in his response. "My friends call me Ben. I'd like it if you called me Ben," he continued.

"I will do just that. Ben, welcome aboard. My friends call me Paul. Since we've just become friends, you can call me Paul. If you need anything during our flight, just push the service button."

Ben took his seat, row one, seat four. After sitting down, he reached up and pushed the service button. Pauline immediately responded. "Is there something I can do for you?" she asked.

"No, no, nothing at all. I just wanted to make sure this thing works," he smiled, "Paul."

"I assure you it works." She tucked a loose strand of hair behind her ear. "Ben. Are you sure there is nothing I can get for you? How about a pre-flight beverage?"

"Ya, know, that sounds super. Do you have any Harveys Bristol Cream over ice?" Ben asked, expecting his request to be too specific to be fulfilled. He'd settle for a nice merlot. "If you do, that would be super."

Pauline smiled and proceeded to the back of the suite. "Dot!" Pauline forcefully whispered. "Dot!"

Dot approached Pauline. "What is it; and why are we whispering?" Dot asked.

"Keep your mitts off one-four. I've got plans for that one!" Pauline joked.

Dot looked over Pauline's shoulder at Ben. "Um, um! He is a

looker, Paul." The two women giggled like schoolgirls. "I'll stay away from one-four if you stay away from two-eight."

Pauline quickly glanced over Dot's shoulder.

"Two-eight, Dot?" Pauline asked. "That old man? He looks like he could keel over any moment!"

"He sure does," Dot agreed, and she winked. "But he looks wealthy! I just gotta get him to propose before we reach Los Angeles." Both ladies covered their mouths to muffle their laughter.

Pauline returned to Ben's seat with a Harveys on the rocks, a warm Snickerdoodle cookie, and a cool lemon-infused washcloth. "I took the liberty of baking what I thought might be your favorite cookie. If there is anything you need..." Pauline looked directly into Ben's eyes. "You obviously know what to do to get what you want." Her subliminal compliment did not escape Ben's attention.

"Well, that would be good, Paul. Real good." Ben took a sip of his Harveys. "I hope you're right!"

CHAPTER FIFTY-THREE
TRICK-OR-TREAT
OCTOBER 31, 1971

The telephone rang, and Ben was quick to pick up the receiver. "A... low?"

"Hi, Ben? It's Cynthia Peterson, your neighbor."

"Oh, yeah. Hi, hiya, Cynthia. How ya doing?" Ben Haughton sat in the chair and crossed his right leg over his left knee.

"Well, that's what I am calling about. Mike and I are down with some kind of bug and wondered—I know it is a lot to ask—we wondered if you would take Kelly around the apartment complex to trick-or-treat."

"Well, ya know, I was planning to go tricker-treating by myself," Ben joked. "But I suppose I could use a partner. Sure, sure, I'd be happy to do that."

"Oh, Ben. Thank you. Thank you so much. I know she will enjoy herself. Thank you."

"No, no, no. Don't mention it. I'll be happy to take her around. I've got absolutely nothing planned this evening, so this will be super, super."

At seven-thirty, Ben made his way across the hall to the Peterson's apartment.

"Trick-or-treat?" Ben shouted as the door opened to Cynthia.

"Where's your bag?" she asked.

"Oh, I don't use a bag. I eat the candy along the way," Ben responded.

They both laughed. Cynthia gave Ben a Snickers candy bar.

"Snickers? Snickers? Those are my favorites." He immediately opened the wrapper and made short order of its contents.

Kelly ran down the hall to the front door. She met Ben with a big hug around his legs.

"What do you say to Mr. Haughton, Kelly?" Cynthia asked.

Kelly looked puzzled. "Trick-or-treat?" she asked.

"No, silly! You need to thank him for taking you trick-or-treating," Cynthia corrected.

"Oh, thank you, Mr. Haughton," Kelly said as she gave him another hug.

Ben Haughton bubbled with excitement as the two of them left her apartment. "Maybe we will get some more Snickers."

Halloween was a mindless, fun time of the year. There was no pressure for gifts and minimal pressure to send cards. However, there was an uncompromising responsibility to pilgrimage throughout the entire apartment complex in search of the perfect trick-or-treat.

Ben considered passing by apartment number 306. He'd heard it had only recently been rented, and he did not want to bother the new occupants. However, Kelly was already making her way to the front door. Before Ben could stop her, she'd pressed the doorbell.

"Trick-or-treat?" Kelly joyfully asked as she held out her bag, awaiting yet another morsel of sugar.

The attractive brunette looked directly into Ben's eyes. "Show me a trick, and I'll give you a treat." Her comment was not meant for Kelly.

Ben recognized the woman, but he could not immediately place where they had met.

Pauline softly spoke, "Mr. Haughton, isn't it? Or can I still call you Ben?"

Ben tried desperately to remember the circumstances of their previous meeting.

"It's a pleasure to see you again. Is this your daughter?" Pauline asked.

"Uh, no, no. This is my neighbor, Kelly. Kelly, say hello to... to, I'm sorry. What is your name again?" Ben stumbled.

"Pauline. My name is Pauline. It is very nice to meet you, Kelly. Mr. Haughton and I met a month or two ago." She glanced up at Ben. "You remember, don't you; Philadelphia to Los Angeles?"

Ben appreciated the clue; it all came back to him—the stewardess.

"Oh, yeah, yeah, Pauline. I remember now. Yea, super, super. Sure, sure, you can call me Ben. I'm surprised you remembered. So, you live here now?"

"I just moved in last week. Come on in if you have a second; please excuse the boxes. I haven't finished unpacking," Pauline said.

"Oh, sure, sure. I've got the same floor plan as your place. Yeah, so... I guess we are neighbors."

"I guess we are. So, what will it be?" Pauline asked.

Ben didn't understand the question.

"What will it be? Harveys? Trick? Treat?" Pauline suggestively asked.

Ben nervously chuckled. "Well, I think Kelly will want a treat if ya have one. I'm good right now."

"That's wonderful. Perhaps you could come back a little later?"

"Yeah, well, that would be good, but I've got Kelly here and... maybe we could get together next week?" Ben suggested.

"I'm flying through Friday," Pauline lamented.

"Well, what about Saturday night? Would you be free on the...," Ben took out his calendar, "the sixth?"

"The sixth? Yes, yes. I would like that very much," Pauline replied.

"What if I come over about six? We'll have a nice dinner and get to know one another." Ben began to chuckle. "Ya know, it's always good to get to know your neighbors."

"Yes, Mr. Haughton. It certainly is." Pauline placed a handful of candies in Kelly's bag. She turned and placed her hand softly on Ben's lapel. "I'll look forward to Saturday night, Ben."

CHAPTER FIFTY-FOUR
DATE
NOVEMBER 1971

Pauline spent the better part of the day preparing for her date with Ben Haughton. The fresh highlights in her pageboy cut perfectly framed her face. Her bangs were just long enough to intentionally cover her left eye, creating a mysterious but playful appearance.

Admiring her hands, Pauline could not help but smile. Beautiful hands were a requirement of TWA stewardesses. The French manicure accentuated her long, soft fingers.

Selecting the proper clothing was important. Pauline wanted to look stylish, independent, and self-reliant without appearing aloof and self-absorbed. Her red jumpsuit might be too bold for a first date. Her polyester knit pants and baby-blue knitted sweater coat would be less commanding—the conservative choice.

Ben did not give fashion a second thought. He wore his long-sleeved white shirt with French cuffs, tan khakis, and navy blue microsuede blazer. It was a simple choice. Pauline would soon realize Ben ALWAYS wore his long-sleeved white shirt with French cuffs, tan khakis, and navy blue microsuede blazer.

At five-forty-five, there was a knock at Pauline's door. She bristled, *Are you kidding me? No one arrives fifteen minutes early to a first date!* She looked out the peephole. Ben had his back to the door—but Ben was good looking from any angle. Pauline's frustration was immediately replaced with panic.

"Just a minute. I'll be right there," she called out from behind the door. She quickly ran back to her bedroom closet.

"Oh, no problem, no problem. I'm a little early, I guess," Ben chuckled.

Within minutes, Ben could hear the latch on the door release and the chain swing free. The door opened. Pauline was stunningly beautiful in her red jumpsuit and black pumps, accented by her matching clutch.

"Oh, wow, wow. You look beautiful," Ben stuttered. "Uh, here, I brought this for you." Ben gave her a single red rose. He was strikingly handsome. Just standing there he exuded a comfortable nonchalant strength.

Pauline was smitten.

"Uh, are you ready to go? I know I'm a little early. I hope I didn't rush you," Ben apologized.

Pauline suddenly realized Ben was still awkwardly standing in the hallway. "Oh, no, no. Come on in. I'll just need to put this in some water and get my coat."

"I thought we could go to a little place I kinda like over on Illinois Street—St. Elmo," Ben said as Pauline turned the corner from her hallway into the kitchen.

"Sounds great. I've never been there before. I like visiting new places." Pauline returned from the kitchen with the rose in a bud vase. "It's beautiful, Ben. Thank you so much."

Ben stepped to the side as Pauline opened the closet door behind him to get her coat.

"Let's go!" I'm ready; let's go!" Pauline did not attempt to hide her enthusiasm.

As they reached Ben's car, Ben swept in front of Pauline and opened her door.

"Oh, my, Mr. Haughton. Are we trying to impress?"

"Would you go out with a man that did any less?"

"Touché. Thank you, kind sir."

"Not at all, *my fair Maiden*," Ben replied.

"What did you say?" Pauline was emphatic. "Ben, what did you just say?"

Ben nervously reran the conversation in his mind, hopeful he hadn't said something to offend his date. "Uh, I said I hope you like the food at St. Elmo?"

"No, no. You said something else; you called me something."

"Uh, I didn't mean anything. I uh, I just opened the door, Pauline." His eyes darted around, searching for a lifeline.

"No, Ben, no. I said, 'Thank you, kind sir.' And you said..." She leaned forward, encouraging Ben to remember.

"Uh, I don't know. I don't remember—really." Ben's concern was clouding his memory. "I just said, *'Not at all, my fair maiden.'*"

Pauline appeared to be in a momentary trance.

"Honest, Pauline. I didn't mean anything by it. I'm sorry..."

"No, please don't be sorry; please. You took me back to a place I'd forgotten. A wonderful place. I am honored to be your fair maiden if you will be my knight in shining armor."

Relieved, Ben turned the key. The Cadillac's engine purred to life. He looked at Pauline. There was a glint in his eye as he playfully bowed his head, "As you wish."

The sunset blazed a million colors through the tears in Pauline's eyes. They were happy tears—they would not fall. These were tears meant to be kept inside with the memories that stirred them. They were warm, loving tears, arising from a peace she'd long forgotten.

Pauline observed Ben's every move. He was the ultimate gentleman. Arriving at St. Elmo, the valet service opened both Ben's and Pauline's doors.

"Here, let me go around and help you out," Ben offered. Pauline attempted to inconspicuously bring her right leg back into the car.

He is so cute, she quietly thought.

Ben stepped in front of the valet, who was still holding the door open for Pauline. He offered his hand and could not help but notice the softness of Pauline's touch. Placing her arm within his, he asked, "Is this all right?"

"It is quite all right, Mr. Haughton," Pauline beamed with satisfaction.

Heads turned as the couple entered the restaurant.

"Good evening, Mr. Haughton," the maître d' greeted Ben—his eyes, however, were focused on Pauline.

"Uh, hiya, hi. I've got a reservation for two tonight. Ya got us down there somewhere?" Ben casually asked, knowing full well the reservation had been made a week in advance and confirmed numerous times throughout the week.

"We have a beautiful table prepared for you, sir. The only thing more stunning is the lovely lady joining you."

Pauline blushed.

Red jumper—right choice, she thought.

"Please follow me," the maître d' led the couple through the restaurant. "I am certain you will enjoy your table this evening, Mr. Haughton. We took extra care to position things precisely to your liking."

"Ah, that's super, super. Thanks, Manny."

"It is always a pleasure, sir."

Pauline was beginning to wonder just how many dates begin at the *Haughton table.*

"It sounds like you're a regular here, Ben," Pauline began to probe.

"Ha, well, yeah. Yeah, as a matter of fact, my family has been coming to St. Elmo since the early 1900s." Ben took a sip of water. "Why change something that's working for you?" Ben's shoulders bounced as he laughed at his comment.

"And do you bring all of your dates here?" Pauline inquired as if kidding—but she was kidding on the level.

"Oh, hundreds," Ben chuckled. "I'm probably keeping the place in business!" His shoulders bounced all the more.

"Oh, really?"

"Nah, nah. This is more of a business place," Ben explained.

Sitting upright, Pauline crossed her arms, tilted her head just slightly, and she closed her right eye. "What kind of *business*?"

"Ah, no, no. You've got me all wrong, Pauline. Nah, I'm not the dating type. This is a first for me in a long time."

"Oh, and why is that?"

"Well, ya know. I was previously married," Ben began. "Marriage is not the best prerequisite for dating." Ben took another nervous sip of water. "I've got two girls who now live in Chicago with their mother. Between visiting them when I can and running a business, there's been no time to date." Ben took advantage of the pause in Pauline's questions. "Let's get something to drink. What would you like?"

"Are we having wine with dinner?" Pauline asked.

"Oh, sure, sure," Ben replied. "I'm going to order a..."

"A Harveys Bristol Cream, right?" Pauline interrupted. "Over ice."

"Yea, yea—hey, how did you know that?"

"Some people we never forget. We remember everything we possibly can about them," Pauline suggestively replied.

Ben appeared oblivious to her subtle compliment.

"So, what will it be?" he asked.

"Since we are having wine with dinner, I'd like a lemon drop."

"Good evening, Mr. Haughton, ma'am. Can I get you two a beverage?" the server politely asked.

"Oh, hiya, hi, Cheryl. This is Pauline, Pauline..." Ben realized he did not know Pauline's last name. "Pauline..." In a panic, he looked to Pauline for assistance.

"Oh, you go right ahead, Benjamin Haughton. I'm kind of enjoying watching you squirm a little."

"What the heck is your last name, Pauline?"

"Why, thank you for asking, Mr. Haughton." Pauline turned to Cheryl. "Good evening, Cheryl. I'm Pauline, Pauline Bianchi."

"THAT'S RIGHT!" Ben attempted to cover not knowing.

Pauline slowly turned her head toward Ben and smiled. "Of course, it's right; I was born with it and have been using it for years." She turned back to Cheryl. "I'll have a lemon drop, sugar around the rim, and two lemon twists, please. Mr. Haughton will have a double Harvey's Bristol Cream over ice."

"Those will be coming right up."

"Hey, Pauline, I usually just get a single Harveys. I..."

Pauline reached forward and touched Ben's lips. "From now on, you'll enjoy a double."

"Well," Ben spoke with the tips of Pauline's fingers gently pressing against his lips. "Can I have a Snickerdoodle with it, too?"

Pauline immediately sat upright. "You remembered! Oh, my goodness! Benjamin Haughton, you did remember me!"

"Well, some people we never forget. We remember everything we possibly can about them." Ben smiled.

There is something very special about this man, Pauline thought to herself.

Cheryl returned with the drinks. "Here you go. We have a beautiful lemon drop for Pauline Bianchi." Cheryl emphasized Pauline's last name, hoping it would reinforce Ben's recall in the future. "A double Harveys Bristol Cream over ice for you, Mr. Haughton. Would you like a few minutes to look over the menu?"

"Yeah, let's do that. Give us some time," again Ben's shoulders bounced ever so slightly. "We probably could use some time to get to know one another."

He lifted his glass in a toast, "Maybe I did hear your name before and forgot, I don't know. But I'll tell you this, I'll never forget the way I felt when you opened the door to your apartment. I hope this is the first of many more times together."

As their glasses touched, Pauline assured her date, "It will be, Mr. Haughton. It will be."

CHAPTER FIFTY-FIVE

SECOND MEETING

DECEMBER 1971

It had been six weeks since Ben had seen Pauline. He and his brother, Hal, boarded flight 132 bound for San Francisco.

The welcoming flight attendant was an attractive blonde. Ben looked at her name badge, Miss Johnston.

"Welcome aboard, Mr. Haughton. My name is Jackie. I will be serving the suite on your trip to San Francisco. Your seat is row one and seat four. Have a wonderful flight."

Hal walked in just behind Ben.

"Oh, my goodness. We have another Mr. Haughton. You will be sitting in row one and seat two, sir. Welcome aboard."

Ben and Hal walked up the aisle and took their seats. A creature of habit, Ben always requested row one and seat four.

The cabin doors were closed, and the familiar greeting came over the public address system:

"Good morning. Welcome aboard flight 132 with service from Chicago to San Francisco. We'll be flying our new Boeing 747-131 at a cruising altitude of 38,000 feet. The weather in San Francisco is going to be a bit warmer than our twenty-four degrees here in Chicago with an arrival temperature in the mid-40s. Radar indicates clear skies ahead, but we do ask that you keep your seatbelts buckled for your comfort and safety as well as the safety of those around you. We've got a great meal planned during our flight, and our beverage service will begin shortly after take-off. So sit back, relax, and if there is anything your TWA Team can do for you, we look forward to serving."

One hour into the flight, Jackie Johnston approached Ben, who was skimming the front page of his *Wall Street Journal*.

"Excuse me, Mr. Haughton. I have a special delivery for you from a friend."

Jackie delivered a double Harveys Bristol Cream and a warm Snickerdoodle.

"Huh? What's this? Who, how did, where?" Ben dropped his paper and looked around.

Jackie smiled and pointed over Ben's shoulder to the curtain separating the suite from general boarding. Peeking through the curtain was Pauline.

Jackie interrupted Ben's interlude, "Excuse me, Mr. Haughton? Miss Bianchi advised me to make the delivery and keep my hands off." She chuckled as she returned to the galley, and Pauline made her way to Ben's seat.

"Pauline! Hey, how are you? You look great! How have you been? Why haven't we seen each other?" Ben's awkward sincerity was amusing.

"Hello, kind sir. Let's see, I'm fine, thank you. I've been well. Because you haven't called." Pauline maintained a forceful, inquisitive expression as she continued to await Ben's response. It was obvious she was not going to leave until she got one.

"Uh, this is my brother Hal. Have you met Hal? Hal, this is Pauline, the gal I told you about."

"Hello, Pauline. It's a pleasure to meet you," Hal politely responded.

Ben continued to stammer, "Yeah, yeah. Well, I've been busy, yeah, real busy. Our business is doing pretty good, ya know. Hal handles the finances, and I handle the manufacturing. Yeah, it's doing pretty good." He paused, trying to remember the question. "Yeah, so that's why I haven't called. We've been really busy."

"I see," Pauline responded, though still not convinced she'd not been forgotten. "And what is your schedule in the coming weeks?" she asked.

"Huh, oh, yeah. Well, Hal and I have business in San Francisco this week, but we will be returning to Indy on Saturday. You flying on Saturday?" Ben asked.

"Schedules are not up yet, but usually I am not flying on the weekends," Pauline replied. "Saturday is Christmas, so it's probably not the best weekend to get together."

"Yeah, yeah. You're probably right. Listen, ya got anything planned for New Year's Eve?" Ben asked.

Pauline glanced over Ben's shoulder to the curtain separating the cabins. "No, Ben. No plans yet," Pauline replied.

"Well, ya want to do something? Ya know, bring in the New Year's celebration together? I mean, we could have dinner or something?" Ben leaned forward.

Hal quietly watched the interaction. Pauline gave a glancing smile at Hal. "Or something would be nice. You still have my number?"

"Sure, I do, sure. I'll call and we'll set something up. Maybe catch a nice dinner at St. Elmo. You liked their food, didn't you?"

"St. Elmo was wonderful, Ben. I will look forward to your call. Excuse me, I've got to return to my station." Pauline turned her attention to Hal. It was a pleasure to meet you, Mr. Haughton."

Pauline disappeared through the curtains.

"What do ya think of her, Hal?" Ben asked his brother.

"What do you mean, 'what do you think of her?' I didn't talk to her. If ya mean, what does she look like? She looks attractive. Other than that, I don't think anything of her." Hal took a long look at his brother. "What do you think of her?"

"Me? Ha! Well, she's a nice girl, nice girl. I don't know. I guess I kind of like her—enough to take her to dinner again. Yeah, yeah. She's a nice girl." Ben tilted his head slightly to the left and was staring at the bulkhead wall when Hal broke his concentration.

"Take it easy, big brother. I've seen that look before and it has always resulted in attorney's fees."

Ben glanced back at Hal. No words were exchanged. Hal adjusted his glasses and shook his head; *or something.*

CHAPTER FIFTY-SIX

CALL FROM SAN FRANCISCO

DECEMBER 1971

"Hello?"

"A... low? Pauline?" Ben's familiar voice sing-songed over the receiver.

"Yes, hello, Ben. I wondered if you were going to call," Pauline dryly responded.

"Of course, I was going to call. I said I would call. Hey, listen. Are we still on for New Year? I'd like to take you out to dinner or something."

"Or something?" Pauline once again suggestively asked.

"Whatever you want to do. I thought we'd go to St. Elmo or something," Ben responded.

"We've been to St. Elmo," Pauline replied. "I'd like to know what the 'or something' is you keep referring to." Pauline's statement seemed to pass right over Ben's head. *Is the man that dense?* she thought.

"Well, St. Elmo is pretty good. Whatever you'd like to do; but St. Elmo always has a great dinner."

Whatever I'd like to do... as long as we eat at St. Elmo, Pauline realized. She forced a smile, "St. Elmo will be fine, Ben. Are you sure you can get us in? It is New Year's after all?"

"Yeah, yeah. I'm pretty sure. We've got quite a history at St. Elmo. I'll give them a call and make all the arrangements. Do you dance?"

"Do I dance? I love dancing, Ben!" Pauline excitedly responded.

"Yeah, well, that's too bad." He chuckled. "I don't dance."

If that was a joke, it wasn't funny. Pauline bristled. "Well then, you just get me to a dance floor, Mr. Haughton. I'm sure I will find someone who does!" Pauline did not attempt to disguise her reservations about Ben's New Year's plans.

"No, no, wait a minute. I don't dance—but I didn't say I won't. Put me in a silk shirt and a pair of bellbottoms, ya never know what might happen! Let's make it a New Year's celebration! Friday, the 31st, New Year's Eve! I'll come by, let's say around six-thirty. Unless you already have other plans?"

Pauline took a deep breath. "Six-thirty will be fine, Ben. Are you still in San Francisco?"

"Yeah, we leave tomorrow morning. It's been a good trip."

"Well, I'm glad to hear it was. I look forward to seeing you—with that silk shirt and those bell bottoms! We're going dancing, Mr. Haughton!"

"Dancing, huh?" Ben chuckled. "Yeah, we'll go dancing. It will be fun; it will be fun. I look forward to seeing you too." Ben hung up the phone.

CHAPTER FIFTY-SEVEN

ENCORE PERFORMANCE, ST. ELMO
DECEMBER 31, 1971

At six twenty-five, Ben made his way from his apartment on the second floor to Pauline's apartment on the third. Having sensed a bit of angst, perhaps created by his early arrival on their previous date, Ben arrived precisely at six-thirty.

Not wanting to be caught off guard, Pauline had been ready since five-thirty.

Pauline answered the door wearing a New Year's party hat and holding a glass of white wine.

"Hey! You started without me," Ben teased.

Pauline put a party hat on Ben and kissed him on the cheek.

"Where have you been, Haughton?"

"We said six-thirty, didn't we?" a confused Ben asked.

"We most certainly did. I just thought maybe you'd come up earlier, and I wanted to make sure I was ready."

"Well, you look ready to me. You look beautiful, Pauline." Ben held his arms out and turned around in a circle, allowing Pauline's review of his attire. "What d'ya think?" Ben asked.

"Paisley silk shirt? Burgundy bellbottoms? Really? Ya went all out, Haughton. Ya went all out." Pauline could not help but giggle.

"Ya want to get going over to St. Elmo, or finish your drink, or pour me one or something?"

Or something... A prospective smile swept over Pauline's face. "Let's go to dinner, Ben. I'm ready."

The maître d greeted the couple. "Happy New Year, Mr. Haughton, Miss Bianchi."

Pauline was impressed. Obviously, Ben had coached Manny. Nevertheless, it was a warm touch to their soiree.

"Hey, Manny. Ya got a table for a couple of stragglers?" Ben playfully asked.

"Mr. Haughton—sir. Stragglers? You must be awaiting a different guest."

He reached forward and took Pauline's hand. "This beautiful lady is anything but a straggler. She, sir, is my welcomed guest."

"Ha, ha. You remember Pauline, don't you?" Ben asked.

"Remember? Mr. Haughton, how could I forget? Miss Bianchi, please allow me to escort you to your table," Manny said.

The attention was overwhelmingly enjoyed by Pauline. She walked to the table with Manny. Ben sauntered behind. She looked back at him and winked in appreciation. Ben wittingly smiled in response.

Manny politely pulled out Pauline's chair, inviting her to be seated. He made certain she was comfortable, took the cotton napkin from her plate, and gently placed it in her lap. "Does madam wish to have this straggler join her?"

Pauline's Jersey accent was all the more accentuated by her melodious response. "Well..., I don't know." She looked at Ben who was still standing behind what he anticipated would soon be his chair. "I was looking forward to a wonderful evening with my knight in shining armor."

The three chuckled and Manny pulled the chair out for Ben to be seated. "Your server will be right with you. Thank you for joining us this evening."

Dinner proceeded as dinner always proceeded at St. Elmo—flawlessly. Pauline kept the conversation going with an array of questions about Ben's daughters and his business. She perceived a heightened sense of involvement and excitement in Ben's responses as he talked about his business. Ben was also accumulating insights about his date.

"So, what is it about your daughters?" Pauline asked.

"What d'ya mean?" Ben asked with an eyebrow raised.

"You don't have much to say about them." Pauline took a sip of her lemon drop, which the bar had prepared without her even ordering. She then repeated herself. "You don't have much to say about them, but you can't stop talking about your business."

Pauline could sense Ben's uneasiness with her question, but it was not Pauline's nature to back down. She continued to probe. "So what is it, Haughton?"

"Ya know, divorce is a tough thing—especially when kids are involved. When you are dealing with two adults it's different. You have an agreement, cut the checks, and go your separate ways, simple. When you've got kids, it sorta messes things up."

"How does it mess things up? You've got kids, they come first. You do what you can to take care of them," Pauline interjected.

"Well, that's true, that's true. I take care of them by running a successful business. They have their own lives with their mother. I don't want to get involved in all that. I see them when I can and call them when I can. Their mother is doing a good job and I don't want to get involved and mess things up. Things are good right now."

Ben could sense the conversation was not heading in the right direction if it was going to end on a positive note, *or something.*

"Things seem to be good for you, but how are they for your daughters? They are still your daughters, ya know," Pauline softly admonished.

"You're right. We've got a good relationship, a good relationship. It isn't easy, ya know. It just isn't easy."

"Well..." her voice faded without continuing. There was nothing more to say. Pauline decided to leave the topic for another time.

"Excuse me," The server interrupted. "Might I bring you the dessert menu?"

"What d'ya say, Pauline? You in for some dessert or something?"

"Or something sounds nice," Pauline responded.

Pauline's double entendre had previously appeared to pass by Ben without him having the slightest inkling the suggestive tease was being offered. This time, however, he simply smiled and called their server back to the table.

"Why don't you just bring us the check? Everything was really good, super. Everything was super," Ben responded.

"The tiramisu and chocolate soufflé are magnificent this evening, sir. Perhaps an after-dinner cocktail to bring in the New Year?"

"No, no, I think we'll just take care of the check. There are a lot of parties going on tonight. We're gonna find one we can crash." Ben looked directly at Pauline. "Or something."

The couple drove back to the apartment complex. Dancing would wait for another evening. Ben escorted Pauline to her apartment. Ben would not see his apartment until the first day of the new year.

CHAPTER FIFTY-EIGHT
WHY WAS SHE SO HATEFUL?

"How long before Ben and Pauline were married?" I asked after taking the last swig of my second cup of coffee.

"It was less than a year. Peggy remembered it starting out a happy marriage. Ben offered Pauline a sizable monthly allowance to resign from TWA. It was not a difficult decision for Pauline. Ben's allowance was better, and the benefits of being a stay-at-home full-time Haughton exceeded anything Pauline could otherwise hope for at TWA.

Pauline enjoyed their time with Carrie and Kathy. Having them around was like a bonus check for Pauline. If there was something she wanted or something she wanted to do, all she had to say was, the girls would like to have this or that, or the girls would like to do this or that, and Ben would respond with cash. The four of them would spend a lot of time at Lake Tippecanoe in the Haughton's lakeside cabin."

"Ha, cabin! That so-called cabin is a spacious three-story compound!" I exclaimed.

"So I've heard," he said as he remembered the description in my book.

"Did Peggy give you any clue why Pauline was so jealous of Carrie? What brought on the hatred?"

"Mr. Dustin, I don't know that she hated Carrie. I don't think it was quite that simple. Her emotions were always in flux. One moment she would be playful, content with all the comforts her husband's company afforded. In the next moment, she would feel threatened by anyone who shared an influence in his life. The girls posed an unintended threat to her future."

"In what way?" I asked incredulously.

"Ben loved his daughters—in Ben's own way. I'm not certain Ben experienced the same emotional bond most people think of as love. His was more mechanical. It was important to maintain his comfort by keeping those closest to him content. Money was a tool to avoid confrontation and a bargaining chip to keep peace.

"Pauline had become dependent on the girls. They were her means of getting what she wanted. It was fine as long as she could continue to use them as a reason to fulfill her desires. However, not everything Pauline wanted could be excused as something the girls wanted or needed. This realization haunted Pauline. Was Ben just being generous toward the girls? Would he be as generous when Pauline requested things for herself?

"Another fear she expressed to Peggy was more long-range— about the future. When Ben passed, the girls would most likely inherit the majority of his estate. It would be, in Pauline's mind, two against one. Pauline feared she would be left with very little and would be expected to depend upon the girls. In Pauline's mind, that would never work."

"So, her hatred, or jealousy, or whatever you want to call it, was unavoidable. I mean, the girls didn't have to do anything. Pauline simply hated them for who they were?" I reasoned.

"Again, you use the term *hate*. It just wasn't that simple. Pauline feared the girls. Although they didn't know it, she was no competition for the power they had over their father. That uncontrollable fear created the hateful responses you refer to. If she truly hated the girls, there would never have been good times."

CHAPTER FIFTY-NINE

THE EARLY YEARS

AUGUST 1972

O n August 11, 1972, Ben Haughton and Pauline Bianchi exchanged their vows and were married by the Monroe County Justice of the Peace. They enjoyed a ten-day honeymoon in the Bahamas.

Returning to Indiana, they contacted Ben's former wife and invited Ben's daughters, Carrie, age thirteen, and Kathy, age ten, to join them at Lake Tippecanoe.

To the casual observer, the Haughton family was tight-knit, fun-loving, and carefree.

"Come on, you guys! The water is beautiful!" Pauline turned and sprinted off the end of the pier.

"Woo-hoo! Oh, my gosh! The water is beautiful—AND COLD! Come on, don't be party-poopers!"

Carrie and Kathy held hands, broke into a sprint, and jumped off the end of the pier into the chilly water of Lake Tippecanoe. Pauline laughed as the two popped up, their teeth chattering in unison.

"We're going to get you," Carrie shouted as she and Kathy swam toward Pauline.

Pauline's splashes slowed the girls' progress, but they finally made it through the walls of water and grabbed hold of their stepmother.

"Okay, okay, you got me!" Pauline gave in. It was her turn to be pummeled by their unending splashes. "Okay, come on you guys. I give! I give. Come on. Let's get some lunch."

Ben stood on the sandy beach, enjoying the entire episode. As the girls exited the chilly water, he gave both a beach towel.

"How was the water, kids?" Ben asked as he handed Pauline her towel.

Pauline responded, "Ya wanna know? Ya wanna know, Dad?" She pulled the towel and grabbed Ben's wrists.

"Come on, girls! Let's show Dad how the water is!"

Ben feigned a struggle, but he allowed the trio to playfully push him into the chilly water. "Oh, no! Look what you guys have done!"

Carrie and Kathy giggled uncontrollably seeing their dad, fully dressed, drenched from head to toe.

"Come on, guys. Let's get cleaned up and get some lunch," Pauline shouted.

As the girls ran across the sandy beach, Pauline took Ben's hand and walked with him to the porch. "You're all wet, Haughton!" she teased as they reached the bottom step.

Ben chuckled. Pauline placed her arms around his neck, and they embraced. Carrie and Kathy peeked through the sliding glass doors, giggling in delight and interrupting Pauline's and Ben's romantic interlude.

"I'm gonna get you two!" Pauline shouted.

Carrie and Kathy stumbled over their towels as they vainly attempted to run up the stairs leading to their bedroom.

"Gotcha!" Pauline grabbed the two wet girls and tickled them mercilessly. They giggled with delight. "Ya had enough? Ya had enough?" Pauline asked as she continued tickling them.

"Enough! Enough!" The girls squealed as they both attempted to catch their breaths.

She gave both girls hugs and helped them dry off.

"Okay, you two," Pauline whispered excitedly. "Let's get cleaned up and make your dad take us someplace real expensive for lunch!"

Pauline brushed and dried their hair, picked out dresses that complimented the jumpsuit she would be wearing, and the three made their way down the stairs.

"Sweetheart? The girls want you to take us out for an expensive lunch. Can we drive to Barbee?"

"Ah, Paul. That's kind of a long way. Don't we have stuff here to make lunch?" Ben asked.

"Ah, but, sweetheart, please. Let's drive to Barbee or someplace and have a nice lunch for them. We'll be making memories." Pauline stroked his hair as she began singing her siren song.

"Gee, Paul. The girls will be just as satisfied with a sandwich or something."

Pauline called for Carrie and Kathy. "Girls, come down here. Tell your dad what you want for lunch." Pauline urged.

"We want something expensive. Daddy, let's go for a ride and get a good lunch," Carrie and Kathy implored.

Ben chuckled. "A good lunch, huh? Peanut butter and jelly isn't a good lunch anymore, I guess, huh?"

"Come on, Dad. We can go for a ride together as a family," Carrie said as she hugged Ben's neck.

"Well, I guess we are going for a ride," Ben said as he got up from his chair. "Let me get a clean shirt on."

"I've laid some pants and a shirt out on the bed for you, sweetheart."

"What's wrong with the pants I've got on?" Ben asked.

"Wear what I've picked out for you," Pauline carefully directed. "Those pants you have on were fine in 1940," Pauline chided.

"Okay, okay, girls. Let me slither into the clothes Pauline has set out on the bed, and we'll go to lunch."

The three ladies cheered.

CHAPTER SIXTY
IT IS ALL I'VE EVER ASKED
1972

Following their first weekend together, the newly established family drove back to Weir Cook Municipal Airport where the girls would board their flight back to Chicago. There was talk of future get-togethers, future trips, and future opportunities to accumulate exciting family memories.

Sitting at the gate brought back memories of how Pauline met Ben. It stirred a brief melancholy longing for her work with TWA. She quietly thought about their slogan, *"You're going to like us."* She realized she truly did. She'd given up a lot in her decision to marry Ben Haughton. She'd also gained a great deal, but on whose terms?

That night, as Pauline and Ben got ready for bed, Pauline commented, "It was wonderful being with the girls. I always enjoy them."

"Yeah, yeah. They're pretty good kids, pretty good," Ben responded. "Their mother's done a pretty good job of raising them, I've got to say that."

Pauline bristled at the mention of Ben's former wife, but she'd leave that for another time.

"Give yourself some credit, sweetheart. You have had some influence on them," she said.

"I suppose; maybe some. It's not like I raised them, though. It's not like we experienced family life, ate together, or traveled together. You know what I mean," Ben said.

"Sweetheart?" Pauline said as she sat on the bed next to Ben. "I want a family."

Ben was not fazed by her comment. "You've got one. You've got me!"

"No, sweetheart. I'm serious. I want a baby, Ben. A child who is ours, just ours. A child we don't have to share with anyone. Our baby. I want a baby, Ben," Pauline begged.

Ben turned and looked at Pauline. "How about a puppy? All we'd have to do is feed it and scoop up its poop and everyone would be happy." Ben laughed at his own suggestion.

Pauline became more animated. "Ben, I'm serious! I don't ask for much and this is something I am serious about. I want a baby."

Ben thought to himself, *you don't ask for much because you have everything you need.*

"Come on, Paul. That's foolishness. What are we going to do with a baby? I don't want a baby now. Not at this age."

Pauline burst off the bed and exploded into a rant the likes of which Ben had never experienced. "You don't want. YOU DON'T WANT! It's always what you want or don't want, Ben. The whole world revolves around you and what you want!"

Ben didn't say a word. He tilted his head slightly to the side as a sick expression developed on his face.

"We're talking about something very important to me, Ben! I want a baby, our baby. A baby we can name, we can raise. A son! A son, Ben! Someone to carry the Haughton name into the future."

"Hal already has three boys. They'll carry the Haughton name into the—"

Pauline interrupted, "I don't care about Hal's boys! I care about ours! I want a baby. Why is it that when the girls want something, you are always ready to give it to them? Huh? I ask for one thing, and you aren't even willing to talk with me about it."

"The girls never asked me for a baby," Ben spewed.

Pauline's venom was on full display. She cursed. "I hate you! I hate you! You're an idiot, Haughton, an idiot! Why did I ever marry you?" Pauline slammed the door as she exited to the living room. It was their first night in their home together—apart.

The next morning Ben sheepishly walked down the stairs. Pauline was at the kitchen sink. "Good morning, Paul," Ben said.

"Is it?" Pauline asked.

"Ya know, I was kinda thinking, thinking about what you said. Maybe, you're right. Maybe we should try to have a baby, you know. It wouldn't be half bad trying."

Pauline turned around to see the Haughton glint in Ben's eyes. She threw her arms around Ben. "Oh, sweetheart! I love you so much. I love you so much! You'll see, you'll see. You will be the best daddy any little boy ever had!"

Ben smiled. He'd averted a confrontation and the possibility he might have had to fix his own breakfast.

CHAPTER SIXTY-ONE
THEY TRIED

"Peggy told me they'd tried to have a child on their own for a few years. When they were unsuccessful, they tried alternative methods. Those also failed. Pauline blamed Ben. She didn't know what it was that he'd done, but obviously, he was incapable of having children—and he didn't seem to care that much about it.

The doctors ran Ben through a battery of tests. Surprisingly, the results of the tests proved conclusively that not only was Ben capable of having children, but his numbers also exceeded that of most men his age."

I was puzzled. "Well, then why—."

He interrupted my questioning. "Only then, did Pauline realize the depth of her mother's vengeful heart. As much as she'd tried to blot that part of her life from her memory, the words of her attending nurse suddenly became crystal clear, *Your baby is beautiful, beautiful and healthy, sweetheart. We're going to help you sleep right now. The doctor will be back to finish, and we will clean you up and take you to your room.*"

Her mother made certain Pauline would never bring shame to

her family again; never embarrass her mother. Pauline was destined to never bare another child." He took a sip of his coffee and waited for my response.

I was dumbfounded. I opened my mouth but was unable to formulate my feelings into words. After several quiet moments, I stuttered, "I always felt there must have been something horrible in Pauline's past to cause her to become the person she was. I never would have imagined." I paused to gather my thoughts. "I never would have imagined this."

He smiled and nodded, "And now you are beginning to understand my reason for sharing these things with you."

My thoughts took me back to the Christmas celebration. Our experience at Ben and Pauline's home now took on a significantly different meaning.

"It all came to a head when we went to their home for Christmas dinner. Look, I had no idea she'd ever had a baby—how would I have known that? Looking back, I suppose I do understand a little better her response to our announcement."

CHAPTER SIXTY-TWO

CHRISTMAS DINNER
DECEMBER 1991

Pauline put on the finishing touches of her holiday makeup when the doorbell rang.

"Ben, the kids are here," Pauline shouted from the master bathroom. "Ben? Did you hear me?"

"I hear ya, I hear ya," Ben shouted back.

"Well then answer me," Pauline demanded.

As she applied her eyeliner, she mumbled under her breath, "Is that asking too much, man? Honestly!" Pauline paused and looked out the upstairs window. "Ben, go get the door. The kids have their hands full. I'll be down in a minute; BEN!"

"Alright, alright. Geeze, Paul. I'll get the door." Ben looked out the window. "They haven't even made it to the walkway." He rummaged around the room. "Hey Paul, do you know where the bells are?"

"The what?"

"The Christmas bells. I want to get the kids in the holiday spirit." Ben, wearing a red stocking cap, peeked around the corner.

"You look ridiculous," Pauline responded. She couldn't help but chuckle. "But you are cute, Haughton. I don't know what I'd do without 'cha. But sometimes I'd like to try..."

Ben giggled as did Pauline. It was a rare moment of playful banter. "Do you mean those old bells on the leather straps from your mom's house?" Pauline asked.

"Yeah, those are the ones. Ya know where they are?"

Pauline responded, "They are in the top drawer of the credenza by the door."

"Okey-dokey. Thanks. I'll go get the door." Ben ambled down the stairs. As he opened the credenza drawer and grabbed the bells, the doorbell rang.

"Ho, Ho, Ho. Merry Christmas. Merry Christmas! Ha, ha, ha, hi, kids, come on in. Come on in. Let me take your coats." Ben paused for a moment, and with a glint in his eye he said, "On second thought, you know where the closet is. Let me take the gifts!"

The three of them laughed and hugged.

"Alright, you guys. What's all the commotion down there?" Pauline jokingly scolded from upstairs. She loved the holidays—all of the holidays. She would spend weeks decorating the house and preparing the menu. But what Pauline anticipated most was family, family sitting around the table enjoying good food and one another.

Pauline made her way down the stairs. She reached the bottom step and turned toward the open door. Ben stepped to the left, and Lonnie to the right, leaving a direct line of sight to Carrie. The Christmas lights in the doorway highlighted Carrie with colors. The light snowfall accentuated Carrie with the reflection of sparkling glitter. Carrie didn't say a word; she didn't have to.

In an instant, Pauline was transported to a place long forgotten —a place she thought she'd forever left in the past. A myriad of emotions collided in Pauline's heart. All she could do was remain transfixed by the beauty and serenity of Carrie, framed in the glistening doorway.

"You're pregnant!" The words exploded from Pauline's lips before she realized what she was saying. She frantically looked at

Lonnie for some sign of confirmation. It was as if she'd been struck with a sudden panic. "Come on, you two!" she begged. "I can tell." Pauline's voice trailed off as if she was in deep thought, "I can tell..."

For such a joyous occasion the entrance to Ben's and Pauline's home became deathly quiet.

Pauline broke the silence, but her tone of voice changed as did her body language. Pauline became rigid. It was as if she'd assumed a defensive posture.

"Carrie, you're pregnant, aren't you?"

Carrie immediately turned her attention to her father, "Merry Christmas, you two. You are going to be grandparents!"

Ben went into shock. The bells fell from his fingertips, making a dull clang on the hardwood floor. "What? WHAT? Really? REALLY?" It took Ben a moment to replay the words in his mind. Once he grasped Carrie's news, he could not contain his excitement. "Oh, my. Oh, my! Can I get you a drink..." The words stuck in Ben's throat. "Can I get you a chair? Are you okay? How do you feel? When is the baby due?"

Pauline could feel her tears well up as she faced Carrie. In a shaky whisper, she said, "I knew it as soon as I saw you." Pauline did not want her emotions to betray her, but she could not hold them back. Without explanation, she turned and quickly walked back up the stairs. Her bedroom door closed behind her. She collapsed on the bed; her body trembled uncontrollably. Her sobs came from a place deep within her soul—a place Pauline thought had been buried never to be exhumed— never to hurt her again.

Pauline would only be a spectator. She felt condemned to face Carrie's and Lonnie's joy—a joy that once might have been hers. Her mind raced back to her pregnancy. She relived every tormenting moment. She could hear her child's adoptive parents say 'It's a boy' just outside the delivery room when Dr. Becker presented her son to them. It was Pauline's son, Pauline's baby! It should have been Pauline's choice—but no.

She remembered the delivery room door swinging shut, the

humming of the monitors, and the muffled conversations outside the delivery room. Pauline heard enough to forever be haunted by an emptiness no person should be condemned to feel.

The minutes passed. As much as she wanted to return to the family, as much as she wanted to share in the Christmas celebration, the pain was too deep. This wasn't her family; it was Ben's. This wasn't her daughter; it was Ben's. This wasn't her grandchild; IT WAS BEN'S!

The bedroom door opened. "Hey, Paul. What's up? The kids are waiting down there to get started."

"I'm sorry. I'm so sorry. I'm..." she paused. "It will take me a few more minutes. I am terribly sorry," Pauline sobbed. Ben took Pauline in his arms.

"Paul, what can I do for you? What is wrong? Is it something I said?" Ben's loving concern added to Pauline's sense of guilt. This gave her liberty to lash out at Ben and, for a moment, free herself of the pain. "Oh, Ben, stop it! It doesn't have to always be about you!"

Pauline pushed her way past Ben and proceeded downstairs. Ben closed his eyes, attempting to replay in his mind what had just happened. Possibly he would then understand why he now found himself standing alone, feeling guilty—of what, he didn't know, but he reasoned he must have done something wrong.

Pauline took a deep breath before entering the kitchen. "Okay, you two. Let's get this dinner started." She was arranging the food on the kitchen island when Ben walked in.

"Oookay. It's time to start carving, I guess," Ben said.

"What better time would there be?" Pauline mocked. "You are such an idiot sometimes." Pauline turned to Lonnie. "Lonnie, help your father-in law-before he hurts somebody."

Lonnie cut the butcher's twine holding the turkey legs together and scooped out the dressing.

"The dressing smells fantastic, Paul," Lonnie said.

"Thank you, sweetheart. I hope it is moist enough."

Pauline then turned her attention and scorn to Ben. "So, carve it already!" Her Jersey accent was all the more accentuated by the shrillness of her voice. "Do I have to tell you everything? Think *for* yourself, not *about* yourself, for a change! Criminy, Haughton!"

The four moved into the dining room. Pauline's Christmas decorations were exquisite. The animated Dickens village was brought to life with the accumulating snowfall just outside the window behind it.

Ben was transfixed by Carrie's news. He wanted to know everything. As plates were being passed and ample portions of turkey, dressing, cranberry sauce, and mashed potatoes were being taken, he continued his questioning. "So, when is my grandson due? Have you felt him move yet? What does that feel like? Have you thought of a name?" He had a strange smile appear on his face, "Benjamin is a good name!" His shoulders bounced as he laughed at his own comment.

Pauline did the best she could to internalize her pain; her visage was stoic. Carrie interpreted it as anger. Little did anyone know Pauline's tormented past ripped at her heart with every question Ben asked. Pain, confusion, loneliness, and loss replaced the Christmas spirit Pauline hoped to have provided for the family.

Pauline could take Ben's torturous questions no longer. "Geez, Ben! You've had two daughters. You'd think you'd never been around a pregnant woman before. Let her eat."

"Huh? What? Geez, Paul. This is our first grandchild." Ben stopped himself from going further. His face suddenly became sullen. "I'm sorry. I, I didn't mean to upset you. I mean, I—"

Pauline interrupted, "Ben, just finish eating. 'I, I, I.' It isn't always about you, Benjamin Haughton. It isn't always about you!"

Pauline fought back tears as she hastily got up from the table, exiting into the kitchen. Ben looked at Carrie. His eyes then glanced at Lonnie. No words were exchanged, but his expression of hopeless perplexity shrouded the remainder of the evening.

As the Dustins backed out of the driveway. Pauline slowly walked back into the dining room. Tears streamed down her cheeks as she quietly sat at the empty table. The Dickens village rested in front of the window just as it had during dinner. It was a peaceful scene. Pauline imagined herself in a different place, a different time. Her eyes strolled down the snow-covered streets within the scene, past Fagin's Hide-A-Way, around the corner where she'd carefully placed The Old Curiosity Shop. As her imagination carried her down the walkway, she turned on Craven Street, pausing only for a moment at 2812, the home of Mr. Brownlow. Her memory took her back to the story of Oliver Twist and the kindly Mr. Brownlow who adopted him.

Adoption.

She looked at the faces of the Dickens characters. She had strategically placed the porcelain figurines throughout the scene. Dancers, sleighs, chimney sweeps, and even a constable were engaged in a festive celebration. In front of St. James Church, the elderly man with his plate of treats sang Christmas carols with four others, whose lanterns illuminate their music in the cool night air. But something —someone—was missing. She recalled a child. A child quietly singing and celebrating. The figurine originally came with the set of carolers, but until that moment, Pauline never recognized it was missing. Frantically her eyes darted from block to block, from scene to scene. The child was not there.

"Paul? Are you alright?" Ben asked.

There was no answer. Pauline opened the doors of the credenza the village display rested on. One by one, she pulled out the empty boxes.

"Paul? Is there something I can help you with? What are you looking—"

"Leave me alone, Ben. Just, just leave me alone!"

Ben nervously finished cleaning what little was left in the kitchen and went up to bed.

Pauline pulled every box from every shelf and drawer. Finally, in the very back, on the bottom shelf, she saw a small white box. It had never been opened. Stamped on the box were the words "CAROLERS —CHILD."

Her hands trembled as she slowly, carefully slid her fingernail under the tape that secured the box. The box seemed to fight against Pauline's attempts to remove the porcelain figurine. Never removed, never part of the celebrations, it remained snuggly locked away, safely forgotten. Pauline held the figurine and gazed upon the little child's features. What might he be thinking? Did this lifeless work of art feel the loneliness of being forgotten?

Pauline was too emotionally drained to climb the stairs. She carried the figurine into the living room and fell asleep holding the porcelain child close to her heart.

CHAPTER SIXTY-THREE
IT ISN'T FAIR
1991

The next morning, Ben awoke and found Pauline still on the living room couch.

"Pauline? Are you alright? Pauline?"

Pauline slowly looked up. She did not speak but reached up and pulled Ben down to her, the figurine still gripped within her hand. "Oh, Ben," Pauline cried in desperation. "Ben, I can't stand the emptiness. I can't go on with this loneliness. The unending pain, the continual wondering—Ben, it's driving me crazy!"

"Paul, what are you talking about?"

"My baby, Ben. The baby I was forced to give up. Ben, Carrie is going to have a baby, a baby! Ben, your daughter is going to have the baby I never got to keep. I'm going to have to see that child for the rest of my life! Ben, it isn't fair! It isn't fair at all!"

"Pauline, Carrie is a young woman. You can't blame Carrie and Lonnie for having a baby."

"Oh, Ben! I'm not blaming them. Listen to me; listen to me! I want MY BABY! I deserve MY BABY! You wouldn't understand. You wouldn't even try to understand. My heart sinks every time I pass a stroller, or a mother holding a baby, every time I hear a baby cry. Ben, my life will be a living hell every time I see your grandchild!"

Ben may not have understood Pauline's feelings, but he realized a living hell for Pauline would also be unending for him. "Paul, what do you want me to do—what can I do? I'm fifty-three years old, Paul! We can't have a child of our own. We know that. What do you want from me?"

"I want to adopt! I want us to adopt a baby; I need to adopt a baby, Ben. I know we are older, but if we offer him love—a love he wouldn't get otherwise if we offer him an opportunity—an opportunity he would never have otherwise if we offer him a name—a successful name, the Haughton name, he will be loved and he will be successful. It's what I want, Ben! Do you hear me? It's what I need!"

Ben thought to himself, *he*?

"Paul, I don't know. I, I don't—" Ben interrupted himself. "Pauline, do you hear yourself? And, what makes you think the baby would be a boy?"

"We would make sure! We would search for a boy, a successor to the Haughton business."

"I have a successor. Carrie is my successor. Carrie is Haughton blood."

"And she will forever end up working for your brother's boys! Face it, Haughton. It's still a man's world at Haughton Manufacturing!"

"But, Paul," Ben stammered.

"You're selfish, Haughton, selfish! It's your way or the highway! It's all about you; it always has been! Why did I ever marry you? I'll tell you what, Mr. Big shot. I file for divorce, and you'll see where your precious money goes! Think about it, Haughton. Do you want it to go to your son or to another ex-wife?" Pauline stormed up the stairs, where she slammed and locked the bedroom door.

CHAPTER SIXTY-FOUR
WHAT DO YOU WANT FROM ME?

"Okay," I said. "Okay. Like I said. Obviously, Carrie and I didn't understand what was going on during that Christmas dinner, but I'll never understand *buying*, as Ben put it, a baby! Sorry, that will never make sense to me."

"I don't blame you. I think you are right. I think it was the turning point in the family relationship."

"Well, it was *a* turning point. I'm not so sure it was *the turning point*." I responded as I remembered the tenor of our get-togethers before Carrie's pregnancy.

"We were on a downhill slide already. Pauline's chronic bitterness was always generously distributed. It became absurd; everyone noticed. I'm sure everyone here noticed it. In Pauline's eyes, St. Elmo represented the Haughton Dynasty. She complained every time we came here. She hated everything about it and everyone involved with it." I took a long sip of the freshly poured cup of coffee in front of me. "Ironic, isn't it?"

"Yes, yes, Mr. Dustin. Her story, and yours, overflows with irony."

"I mean, she hurt so many people; so many! You're sharing this sad story with me, and believe me, I agree. It's about as sad a story as anyone could imagine, but I'm not sure how you expect me to respond. To be perfectly honest, I don't feel any differently toward Pauline than I did before we talked. Listen, it was her jealousy, her greed that hurt my wife, my sister-in-law, a dedicated group of employees, their families, and even Teddy for that matter. I mean, she ruined any chance of him ever being normal, or for any of us to ever enjoy family."

"Mr. Dustin, I've told you. I don't expect anything from you. I'm just sharing. I'm not taking anything away from what you wrote or how you feel."

"I don't know. I mean, Ben buys a baby. Rather than the baby solving anything, Pauline becomes more hateful, more hurtful. Maybe she was frustrated she couldn't return him for a different model!" I sarcastically commented. "She specifically raised Teddy to be every bit as ruthless as she was. And I'm supposed to end the story with *everyone living happily ever after*—right?"

"Hardly," he said. "Look, I can appreciate your sarcasm. No one lives happily ever after in this story."

"Yeah? Tell that to Teddy."

"I know." He took his sip and allowed his eyes to glance over the heads of some other patrons. "It's hard to believe—oh, don't take that the wrong way. I do believe you—it's just a hard reality to have to swallow; to have to accept."

I took a deep breath. "The sad thing? With all the effort she invested into hurting others, she was never happy in return."

"But you and Carrie had a daughter, not a son. Didn't that ease the tension a bit?" he asked.

I abruptly chuckled. "You might think so, but in Pauline's mind, Carrie and I didn't have a daughter. Carrie and I had another Carrie, another Haughton, another competitor, another threatening heir to the Haughton inheritance. Our child was Haughton blood— someone Pauline could never be—someone Pauline would never bring into the world."

As if purposely changing the course of our conversation, he

changed the subject back to Pauline's sister. "Peggy and I continued visiting from time to time after Teddy was adopted. Every time we talked, she'd tell me how conflicted Pauline was. She wasn't happy with Ben, but she wasn't happy without him. She had contempt for you and Carrie, but she missed family when you weren't around. I guess you could say she grew to have the same contempt for Teddy —I suppose you're right. I mean, when you think about it, any parent who would raise a child to fulfill their selfish agenda, to use him as a tool for personal gain, who would take their child down such a hateful and destructive path, couldn't have a real love for the child."

He replaced a piece of bacon that had slipped from his cold burger back into place. He had hardly eaten any of it. He began to chuckle. "Peggy told me precisely what you were saying. Pauline hated, I mean really hated, the repeated dinners at St. Elmo. It wasn't the restaurant. It was Ben! Ben was getting his own way—AGAIN! To hear Peggy tell it, *'Pauline, hated the dark wood, she hated the noise, she hated the menu, even the patrons.'* He took a last bite of his burger. What had been a light chuckle became a hearty laugh, "As a matter of fact, Peggy emphasized Pauline's animosity toward having the same server waiting their table every time they went."

"They were a sad couple. Honestly, it makes me feel sad. They had everything money could afford and were absolutely miserable. Even the joy of adopting a son was temporary. She taught him to turn on everyone only to become a victim of his contempt." I shook my head as he continued to tell the story.

CHAPTER SIXTY-FIVE
HE'S TOO SMART
AUGUST 11, 1997

Wilson Elementary was rated one of the top elementary schools in Indiana. Mrs. Taylor was an inspiring educator. She was known for her ability to motivate young students, conveying within them a desire to learn, a love for education, and a willingness for even the shyest of students to openly discuss their lessons in class. Her skills earned her the lifetime distinction, Teacher of the Year, by the Indiana Department of Education. But Mrs. Taylor had never met Pauline Haughton or Teddy, her son.

"Good morning, Mrs. Haughton. Welcome to Wilson Elementary. I'm Silvia Taylor."

"And my son is Theodore Haughton. You should be introducing yourself to him," Pauline retorted.

The opening confrontation created only a brief pause by the seasoned professional. "Theodore, or do you like to be called Teddy?"

Teddy did not respond. He offered only a disquieting sneer.

"Well, if you don't mind, I'd like to call you Teddy," Mrs. Taylor continued.

"He is an exceptionally bright boy, Mrs. Taylor. I do not want him held back by the other children. Do you have experience teaching gifted children?" Pauline snapped.

It had been years since Mrs. Taylor experienced a formal interview by an aggressive, domineering parent. She assessed the situation and responded. "Mrs. Haughton, I believe all of our children are gifted. As educators, it is not only important that we transmit a prescribed lesson plan, but also equally important we appraise their instinctive talents and guide them in their development."

"Have you ever worked in a manufacturing facility, Mrs. Taylor?" Pauline asked, ignoring Mrs. Taylor's previous response.

"No, Mrs. Haughton, I have not."

"Then how will you," Pauline paused to overemphasize the word, "*guide* my son? He is going to be the owner of Haughton Fabrication."

Mrs. Taylor smiled and directed her attention at Teddy. "Is that what you are going to be, Teddy?" Mrs. Taylor asked.

Once again, Teddy did not respond. His glare troubled Mrs. Taylor. She thought it was indicative of a child in conflict. "Well, congratulations, Teddy. I'm sure whatever you grow to be, you will be successful," she politely concluded.

"Perhaps you didn't hear me," Pauline sternly interjected. "He will be the president and owner of Haughton Fabrication."

Mrs. Taylor's posture stiffened as she directed her attention to Pauline. "Mrs. Haughton, I fear we have started on the wrong foot. I intend to offer your son my years of experience, my record of success, and my unwavering focus on who he is—today. Who, and what he becomes in the future will be greatly influenced by you and by others who impact his life outside the safety of an educational environment."

No other words were spoken. Pauline abruptly took Teddy by the hand and made her way to the administrative office.

"Excuse me! Excuse me—you!" Pauline's discourteous interruption took everyone in the office by surprise. "I want to talk to the principal of this school, and I want to talk to him now!"

The administrative assistant hesitantly approached Pauline. "Ma'am, if I could have your name and the nature of your request, I will let Principal Warrick know you are waiting to speak with him."

"You must be confusing me with someone else. I am waiting to see no one!" Pauline shouted.

A slight smile broke the otherwise expressionless features of Teddy.

"Ma'am, if I could please have your name-"

"My name is none of your business! I am here to talk to the principal of this school!" Pauline was about to continue her rant when the principal's door opened.

"Ladies, ladies. What is going on here?" Principal Warrick inquired.

"Are you the one in charge here?" Pauline barked.

Principal Warrick chuckled, "At times, I am." Judging his assistant's defensive posture and the combative expression on Pauline's face, he judiciously continued, "Evidently, today might not be one of those times."

"My name is Pauline Haughton. This is my son, Theodore. Your so-called 'Teacher of the Year', Mrs. Taylor, was extremely condescending and had the nerve to openly belittle my son!"

Principal Warrick's face contorted with disbelief. "I see. Mrs. Haughton, might I speak with you in my office?"

Pauline scowled at the assistant as she moved Teddy through the swinging half door separating visitors from administrators.

"Uh, pardon me, Mrs. Haughton," Principal Warrick interrupted. "My meeting will be with you. Miss Garland has some wonderful books and games to keep Theodore busy while we visit."

"Uh, pardon me, Principal Warden."

Principal Warrick immediately recognized Pauline's intentional gaff for what it was.

"That's Warrick ma'am, Warrick."

Pauline dismissively flipped her wrist. "Whatever." She then continued, "This is his life, and he has a right to be involved in any discussion about him and any decision that is made about him. Teddy will join us in our meeting, or we will not have a meeting at all!"

"Ah, I see. In that case, have a nice day, Mrs. Haughton. It has been—an experience." Principal Warrick smiled, gave a polite nod, and returned to his office.

This pattern repeated itself throughout Indianapolis and its three remaining elementary schools. In each case, Teddy watched intently as his mother systematically dismembered teachers and administrators alike with her razor-sharp tongue.

"Listen to me, sweetheart. Don't ever let anyone tell you what you will do or won't do. No one, no one will ever take away what is rightfully yours! You understand Mommy, don't you? No one! Mommy is going to find you the perfect school. You are too smart for any of these public school teachers anyway."

Having exhausted any opportunity for Teddy to attend a public school, Pauline turned her attention to private schools. The more expensive, the more exclusive—the better.

The meeting with Mr. Osman was scheduled for Thursday, July 23, at eleven a.m.

Minton School of Achievement was one of the most prestigious junior schools in the nation. There was nothing *elementary* about Minton, and the educators there were quick to correct anyone who mistakenly compared them to an elementary school.

MSA required a full background check of prospective students and their parents. Each prospective student was privately interviewed and tested to determine their potential qualification for acceptance. Only young minds who were thirsty for knowledge, advanced in computation and comprehension skills, socially adept, and with keen athletic skills were viable candidates for the Minton

School of Achievement. Or... prospective students whose parents possessed a sizable bankroll.

"Good morning, Mrs. Haughton. It is a pleasure to welcome you and Theodore to the Minton School of Achievement. Can I get you a cup of coffee?" Miss Bettencourt asked.

"Thank you. That would be very nice. Cream and sugar, please," Pauline responded.

"And for young Mr. Haughton?"

"Would you happen to have hot cocoa?" Pauline asked.

"Absolutely! Some of the finest hot cocoa anywhere. Just one moment."

Miss Bettencourt brought Teddy his cup of hot cocoa. "Please be careful, Mr. Haughton. This cup may be very hot."

Teddy swelled with pride being called Mr. Haughton and receiving his hot cocoa before his mother was served her coffee.

"I do hope you don't mind whipped cream on your cocoa, Mr. Haughton. I always like a little whipped cream on mine," Miss Bettencourt giggled.

"And here is your coffee, Mrs. Haughton. I took the liberty of adding the cream and sugar. I trust it is to your liking."

"Thank you, Miss Bettencourt. It is perfect," Pauline responded.

Teddy took a cautious sip. "This is terrible! It is too cold."

"Oh, my goodness. We can't have that! I am terribly sorry. Please allow me to get a fresh cup for you. I'll make certain it is warmed properly."

As Miss Bettencourt left the room, Teddy glanced up at his mother. Pauline smiled and gave an approving nod. Teddy was learning.

"Here you go, sir. See if this cup is to your liking," Miss Bettencourt offered.

"It's better," Teddy said without the slightest hint of enthusiasm.

Pauline followed Miss Bettencourt into the Chancellor's chamber while Teddy was ushered by Miss Winfrey, the administrative assistant, into the adjacent testing facility.

"Chancellor Osman, thank you so much for giving us this opportunity. There would be nothing more rewarding than to have Teddy attend Minton. He's a gifted child—you'll recognize it immediately."

"Well, Mrs. Haughton, the faculty serving within these halls at Minton School of Achievement are a collective of highly qualified, experienced, and successful educators. They command the collaborative cooperation of families fortunate enough to successfully complete our rigorous schedule of application, who are, shall I say, a more affluent, influential assemblage of society."

For the first time, Pauline felt a tinge of apprehension. Chancellor Osman would not be conquered by flattery.

"Chancellor Osman, I need not recite for you the successes and contributions the Haughton family has, for generations, brought to Indiana. Teddy is the fourth generation to proudly carry the Haughton name."

"So I've read, Mrs. Haughton. So I've read. However, being an heir to the past does not guarantee success in the future."

"You are so right! I couldn't agree with you more," Pauline gushed. "It is precisely why my husband and I have purposed within our hearts to give Teddy the very best education available here at Minton—regardless of the cost."

While Pauline continued her interview with Chancellor Osman, Teddy's frustration was mounting in the adjacent room. Testing angered him. Testing was an unnecessary challenge to what he already knew about himself, what he'd always been told—he was brilliant!

Having completed and reviewed the battery of tests, Teddy and Miss Winfrey made their way to the chancellor's chamber. Miss Winfrey carried the manilla folder containing Teddy's fate. He'd failed every discipline. It was obvious to Miss Winfrey, Teddy was incapable of comprehending the simplest instructions. He was an angry, troubled young man, teeming with arrogance unbefitting a boy his age.

"Chancellor Osman, my husband and I would like to offer the

school a generous donation," Pauline announced as Miss Winfrey and Teddy entered Chancellor Osman's chamber.

"Here are Mr. Haughton's test results, sir," Miss Winfrey announced as she handed Teddy's file to Chancellor Osman. He reached for his reading glasses and opened the file. The results were undeniable.

Teddy's scores were abysmal. Chancellor Osman glanced over his glasses at Pauline, who was signing her donation check. Although he was reading the check upside down, he was able to count the number of zeros. The check was in the amount of ten thousand dollars. He carefully considered the circumstances before speaking.

Pauline slowly, stealthily extended the check toward Chancellor Osman.

"Well, well, well. Congratulations, Mr. Haughton. You have done quite well, quite well indeed." He furtively reached out to accept the donation and continued. "The Minton School of Achievement is honored to open its doors of education to you and the Haughton family. You will be a splendid addition to our school."

Teddy continued his junior and middle school education at MSA. With each issuance of MSA's academic or citizenship probation notice, of which there were many, came the issuance of a generous donation, expunging any such notices from Teddy's academic transcripts.

He didn't go to high school; why should he? He would only carry with him the scorn he'd already so dispassionately gained from his peers. He was a Haughton. He was to be the future owner of Haughton Fabrication—destined.

CHAPTER SIXTY-SIX

IT WAS EVIDENT

Lonnie recalls, "I remember Ben and Pauline pulling Teddy out of the school system. The idea was unthinkable to Carrie and me," I interrupted. "Make no mistake about it, Teddy was gifted; everything he'd accumulated was a gift." I sarcastically told him as I, once again, shook my head in disbelief.

He shook his head in a mirrored response to my disdain.

"Teddy only had two remaining obstacles preventing the total control Ben and Pauline were training him to take. The control Teddy now believed he was entitled to." I paused wanting to make certain he realized I was not referring to Carrie, or her sister Kathy. "In Teddy's mind, the two obstacles keeping him from total control were his mother and father. True, his father gave him everything he'd demanded. True, his mother taught him the power of manipulation and the savagery of a heartless, sharp tongue. But it is also true they had become symbols of authority, previously inconspicuous to Teddy. In Teddy's mind, they too needed to be eliminated by the very deception and greed they'd so purposefully instilled within their son. That is why there was no remorse for the passing of his father and no effort to console or support the livelihood of his mother. He simply seemed to vanish, taking with him the inheritance of his sisters, and the remaining fortune, left by his father for Pauline."

He did not respond, instead, he continued to stir a portion of ketchup that remained on his plate.

I pushed myself away from the table and folded my napkin in an attempt to bring the conversation to a close.

His eyes revealed a noticeable sadness. It was a look of deep regret.

Not wanting to end the meeting on a low note, I awkwardly continued.

"Look, thanks again for purchasing my book and for the invitation to get together and talk."

He didn't respond. He appeared lost in thought. I attempted to soothe any misgivings he might have had.

"Life isn't a problem for her anymore," I said with resolve.

"No, no it isn't," he quietly responded.

As I began to get up from my chair, he put up his hand as if to stop my rising.

"Before you go, there's one more thing I'd like to share with you."

"One more thing?" I asked, thinking the discussion had already slipped into repetitious drama.

"Yes, yes, Mr. Dustin. I would like to share with you the circumstances surrounding her final moments."

"Her final moments?" I asked. I thought to myself, h*ow would you know about her final moments?*

His eyes that only moments before exhibited sad regret suddenly stared directly through me in firm resolve.

"I was the last person to visit with her. I was there when she died."

"You? I thought Carrie and I were the last people to visit her. As a matter of fact, I thought we were the only people to visit her." I sat back down and pulled myself up to the table.

CHAPTER SIXTY-SEVEN

HOSPITAL VISIT
NOVEMBER 12, 2022

He resumed his story during their final moments...

"Excuse me; excuse me, nurse? How is she?" I asked as the nurse exited Room 312.

"The doctor will be here in a moment." The nurse's gentle touch on my arm relayed the message she could not give.

"Thank you." I resolutely stated.

For the next ten minutes, I sat outside her room. I'd thought about what I would say when we finally met. I never thought our meeting would be here. What would I say now? What should I say? Would she even hear me? Would she understand? If this was my only opportunity, I had to communicate, somehow. I had a promise to keep.

When the doctor arrived, he said, "Hello, I'm Doctor Felton. I understand you're a member of the family?"

I paused before answering. It was the first time anyone acknowledged me as a family member. "Yes, Doctor. Yes, I suppose I am. How is she?"

"I'm very sorry. We are doing our best to keep her comfortable, but it is only a matter of time now. How much time—we really can't say."

Time! Time was now the enemy. So much time was already lost, and like the last vestige of sand slipping through an hourglass, its passing seemed to unmercifully increase.

He said, "You can go in and visit with her if you wish. She may not be able to communicate but that doesn't mean she won't be aware of your presence. It will be good for her."

I walked through the open door, into her room, and stood alongside her bed. An array of tubes stretched from her motionless body to monitors surrounding the head of her bed. The nurse stepped in behind me.

"Have there been very many visitors?" I asked.

"Not many, sir. A couple came a few hours ago." She paused as if wondering how a person could be so forsaken. "They were the only visitors I know of since she was admitted five days ago." She stepped to the monitor. "I just need to make a little adjustment. It will only take a moment. Then you can have some privacy." She pulled at the light blue curtain, momentarily separating herself and her work from me. In a matter of seconds, she pulled the curtain back, smiled, and left the room, closing the door behind her.

Pauline and I were alone.

It was a private room. Its window framed a beautiful view of the lake. The room was spacious but uncomfortably cold, sanitized with emptiness. A television hung from the wall, a recliner and coffee table were situated by the window. None of the room's accommodations would be enjoyed. *It was a matter of time.*

As quietly as I could, I pulled a chair to the side of her bed.

"Can you hear me?" I was fighting back tears as I took her hand. She looked so frail. Who would guess this helpless soul could have had such a tortured life? Who would imagine the impact she had on the lives of so many others?

"If you can hear me, squeeze my hand."

I wondered, *was it hopeful imagination or did I feel a momentary twitch?*

I repeated myself. "I'm going to squeeze your hand, and I want you to squeeze mine back." I gently squeezed. The response was unmistakable. It was faint, but Pauline's desire to communicate with me could not be denied.

Thank you, Jesus! I thought.

"I'm so happy to be with you, but I'm so sorry it's here." I attempted to offer a light chuckle. "We're just going to have to get you up and outta this place."

Both sides of Pauline's mouth twitched in a slight smile, but her head appeared to move back and forth as if to knowingly acknowledge there would be no leaving.

"Well, you'll forgive me if I do my best to try," I said as I patted her hand.

Her smile was more definite, and she lightly patted my hand. Pauline was fully aware of my presence.

"I have a message for you. It's a message from a childhood friend of yours. It's a message he asked me to give you."

I took a deep breath.

"Do you remember Alonzo Ricci?"

Pauline's eyes immediately opened. The sudden change in her features startled me. There was an intensity in her gaze. Her eyes begged for more.

"You do remember!"

Pauline squeezed my hand.

"I found him several years ago. I found him through DNA testing." I began to nervously chuckle. "You can imagine what a shock it was."

I paused once again, trying desperately to remember the words I'd rehearsed these past few years.

"It was the reason for my coming to Indiana. It was the reason I searched for you, my reason for moving here—working here."

She gave me a reassuring smile as she began to put the puzzle pieces together.

"He was a good man—a pastor. When I met him, he accepted me with open arms." I then gently held her hand in my two hands and looked up at the ceiling, holding back the tears welling in my eyes.

It was a forced chuckle, "Ha! Can you imagine? His first DNA match and it was me—*his son!* A son he'd never known he had."

"They all accepted me, ya know—the family, the church. He was compelled to openly share his story, our story, with his congregation. They all accepted him, too. He never knew you were pregnant. He never knew I was born. He told me you were the only girl he'd been with before his marriage. He regretted losing touch with you when you suddenly moved away. He finished his schooling and followed in his father's footsteps."

She gripped my hand tightly and stared at my face as if memorizing my every feature.

"He wasn't well when I met him. I was fortunate to have had the opportunity to visit with him several times before he passed. I told him about my family, my upbringing, and what a blessed life I enjoy. I shared with him stories about my parents, they too were believers who loved me and provided everything a young man could ever hope for."

I gripped her hand slightly harder; perhaps out of passion, perhaps out of fear. Reluctance swept over me. A reluctance I had to overcome—I could tell time was fleeting—I had a promise to keep.

"He begged me to look for you. He told me when I found you, I was to give you this message. I was to tell you not to fear, not to regret, not to doubt, but to follow Jesus. He told me these precise words, *'You were always intended, elected, to be His child. When you elect to turn to Him, He will be there welcoming you with open arms.'* Mother? Are you secure in Jesus's love?"

Tears streamed from Pauline's eyes. She softly whispered the word as if she'd never heard it before, *Mother.*

"Mother, it is never too late—never. Right now, right this

moment you can know that you are secure in Him. He did all the work when He overcame sin for us and died in our place on Calvary. He sealed that finished work by conquering death and rising from the dead. Death has no more sting, no more pain, no loneliness, no failure, no remorse. The Apostle Paul said, 'For me to live is Christ and to die is gain.' When we stand before Him, we stand complete, fulfilled—forever!"

My words were familiar to her. She'd heard them every Sunday morning at First Reliance Baptist Church—this time, however, it was different. This time she did not struggle to ignore the words. There were no hats to count, no distractions, nothing to capture her attention and ignore the message. This time the truth of Jesus's love, His soul healing, spoke more clearly, more truthfully, and more powerfully than her words of self-condemnation. This time her heart heard. My mother was finally free.

Peace filled the room.

She appeared to slip back into a quiet slumber. In those fleeting moments, her heart was changed, as were her jealous, selfish, and self-centered desires.

I sat with her for a time—I'm not sure how long it was. I wasn't willing to let go of her hand. I watched as her oxygen levels decreased, and her breathing became shallower.

Suddenly, her visage was altered. Her peaceful slumber had been interrupted by a countenance of deep concern. I could feel her grip tighten. She attempted to pull me closer. The moment seemed to abruptly carry with it a weight of immeasurable conviction. I leaned close enough to feel her last breath on my cheek and hear her last word.

"Teddy!"

The buzzing of the monitors was deafening. I slipped away from her room as nurses hurriedly arrived in response to the droning of the machines.

CHAPTER SIXTY-EIGHT
SAYING GOODBYE
JANUARY 2023

He quietly breathed as he concluded his retelling. His shoulders sank and all the sound seemed to be pressed into the floor under the weight of his brief silence. He softly spoke, "I suppose Teddy took care of the funeral arrangements—although he made no effort to be in attendance. A hand full of mourners arrived at Holy Trinity Cemetery to pay their last respects. There was no minister, no service, no memorial, no celebration. It seemed coldly mechanical. Interment was at two o'clock.

"I thought I'd placed the single red rosebud inconspicuously behind Teddy's garish spray—my arrival and abrupt departure was noticed only by the funeral director serving as the officiant. The rosebud would have gone unnoticed."

His sight penetrated the tears that were dammed by an invisible wall, preventing them from escaping.

He blinked and repeated himself. "It was intended to go unnoticed. I never expected you and Carrie to discover it or to read the note I'd tied to its stem."

Mother,

When I found you, my heart overflowed with emotions. I wanted to thank you for loving me enough to let me go. I wanted to remove any regrets you might have had, any guilt you may have suffered for giving me up. Each time I saw you my heart leaped with gratitude.

When you spoke of your son, I imagined you speaking of me. As much as my heart longed to reveal myself, I couldn't selfishly pursue you, I couldn't selfishly compete with the young man you were raising. This time, it was me who had to let go of you.

But I loved you from a distance.

Though I say goodbye, I say it with the assurance we will meet again. You will always be the one who brought me into this world, and I will always be your son.

With love,
Bennet

EPILOGUE

"So, you see, I had to call. I had to talk with you. I owed it to my mother, to complete her story, her sacred thread. Mr. Dustin, it isn't an excuse, it is an exhibit of God's love. Life is messy. It was messy for the thief on the cross next to Jesus who requested, *'Lord, remember me when you come into your kingdom.'* There was no time to amend his sins, no time to apologize or make restitution. There was no time to *tie up loose ends.* Time was quickly fading away. But Jesus's response to him was personal—a promise, *'Today you will be with me in paradise!'*" Bennet took one last sip of water. "My mother made it!" He shook his head and chuckled. "She made it just before the buzzer, mind you—but she made it—and I have full assurance I will see her again."

I'd long stopped taking notes. The words Bennet shared were seared upon my heart. There was no need for notes; I would never forget. "Bennet, thank you. Thank you for sharing this with me. You've made it impossible to conclude my story without sharing Pauline's."

I struggled to wrap my mind around his story, but I knew that I was meant to hear it.

I said, "I can't help but believe, despite the pain and suffering, somehow, in God's infinite plan, this was how it was supposed to end—oh, don't get me wrong, not that He planned the journey. But I believe He's brought it to an appropriate close."

He remained silent.

"Bennet, I can't help but wonder, how many will be touched by Pauline's redemption? How many will read about her childhood experiences and recognize the devastating entanglements they, unintentionally, may be creating for their children? How many will consider the consequences? What church leaders will be led to reexamine their motives—the purposes of their callings, the consequences of their words, and their actions? Perhaps, just perhaps, Pauline's story will touch the hearts of many who would otherwise be headed on a destructive course for themselves and for those to whom they minister."

It was late, much later than I'd intended on staying. I motioned to our server to bring the bill.

"Mr. Dustin, I'll get this," Bennet insisted.

"No," I replied. "No, Bennet. Thank you for helping me recognize the importance of the words I speak, the actions I take, and the stories I write. Thank you for helping me look past a person's outward actions. Thank you for encouraging me to be more understanding, forgiving, and Godly—considering others' hearts and my responsibility to love as Christ loves."

The conversation ended. The bill was paid. We made our way, between the bar and tables, to the front door.

I felt the need to know one more thing. "Bennet?"

"Yes, sir?"

"Don't get me wrong; I have no desire to find him. Do you have any idea what has happened to Teddy?"

ACKNOWLEDGMENTS

I want to express my never-ending love and admiration for my bride. She has endured, and overcome challenges a mere mortal could not have survived. She has relived many of those challenges within the pages of *The Haughtons: Adoption of Evil*, and now in the pages of *Pauline*. Through it all, she has encouraged me to continue writing. My daughters have been continued sources of inspiration and encouragement. They have been my strongest marketing arm in the distribution of the Haughton trilogy.

A very special thank you to two dear friends, Judy Lynn Kiersey and Faith Harris, whose continued support and promotion have been a source of strength.

To every individual who has purchased my writings, to every book club, luncheon, and store inviting me to speak and sign books, to Jo Peek and Megan Scott who have graciously promoted me in their publications, I sincerely thank each one of you.

To my editor, Stacey Smekofske, thank you for your coaching, your artistic selections in design and formatting, your expertise for making me appear far more talented than perhaps I am, and to your husband and family who have so often sacrificed their time with you, thank you.

Lonnie Dustin

ABOUT THE AUTHOR

Lonnie Dustin briefly attended Bible College and seminary—his intention was to become a Christian minister. His ministry, however, would never be from a church pulpit. Lonnie excelled in business. His advancements and corporate experiences placed him in high-level negations throughout Europe, China, Japan, and along the Pacific Rim.

"God often speaks to us through life experiences. Unfortunately, we too often react to life's experiences rather than allow ourselves time to understand the complete lessons God is attempting to teach."

And so it is that Lonnie has adapted his storytelling techniques to intertwine life experiences with hidden truths. He captures readers' attention, guides them through life events, and encourages his readers to pause, watch for the unseen, and listen with their hearts.

It is, in effect, his ministry.

COMING SOON

Victim or victor? Look deep into the mind of a psychopath. Watch how Teddy stealthily maneuvered his way through life without responsibility or penalty for his actions.

Hated by all who knew him, Teddy wore his pride and position as a badge of honor. No one and nothing would get in his way. He was dangerous—but the greatest danger he would cause would ultimately be to himself!

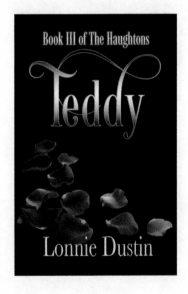

CPSIA information can be obtained
at www.ICGtesting.com
Printed in the USA
JSHW080753160623
43025JS00002B/4/J

9 781958 314067